The Accelerated High School

CORWIN
PRESS

The Corwin Press logo—a raven striding across an open book—represents the happy union of courage and learning. We are a professional-level publisher of books and journals for K–12 educators, and we are committed to creating and providing resources that embody these qualities. Corwin's motto is "Success for All Learners."

The Accelerated High School

A Step-by-Step Guide for Administrators and Teachers

Carrie Baylard Eidson
Edward D. Hillhouse

Foreword by Henry M. Levin

CORWIN PRESS, INC.
A Sage Publications Company
Thousand Oaks, California

For information:

Corwin Press, Inc.
A Sage Publications Company
2455 Teller Road
Thousand Oaks, California 91320
E-mail: order@corwinpress.com

SAGE Publications Ltd.
6 Bonhill Street
London EC2A 4PU
United Kingdom

SAGE Publications India Pvt. Ltd.
M-32 Market
Greater Kailash I
New Delhi 110 048 India

Printed in the United States of America

Library of Congress Cataloging-in-Publication Data

Eidson, Carrie Baylard.
    The accelerated high school: A step-by-step guide for administrators and teachers / by Carrie Baylard Eidson, Edward D. Hillhouse.
        p. cm.
    Includes bibliographical references.
    ISBN 0-8039-6639-3 (cloth: acid-free paper)
    ISBN 0-8039-6640-7 (pbk.: acid-free paper)
    1. Educational acceleration—United States. 2. Socially handicapped youth—Education (Secondary)—United States. 3. High schools—United States—Administration. I. Hillhouse, Edward D. II. Title.
    LB1029.A22 E53 1998
    373.139—ddc21   98-8898

This book is printed on acid-free paper.

98 99 00 01 02 03 10 9 8 7 6 5 4 3 2 1

Editorial Assistant: Kristen L. Gibson
Production Editor: Diana E. Axelsen
Editorial Assistant: Lynn Miyata
Typesetter/Designer: Rebecca Evans
Cover Designer: Marcia M. Rosenburg

Contents

Foreword

When Carrie Eidson left a voice message on my answering machine in the autumn of 1996 and asked me to return her call about her Accelerated High School, my curiosity was whetted. Although the Accelerated Schools Project was in its 11th year at that time and had comprised about 1,000 elementary and middle schools in 40 states, it had no official high school component. I returned her call as soon as I received the message and started firing away with questions. Dr. Eidson was forthcoming in giving the reasons for establishing the high school, and she explained enthusiastically to me how successful it had been in engaging students who were seriously at-risk of dropping out. Furthermore, she told me that they had combined the Accelerated Schools process with that of Caring Communities, a way of addressing the social and health needs of students and their families. I was quite familiar with Caring Communities at the elementary school level, but what Dr. Eidson described was truly innovative and combined the two processes for adolescents.

I begged Eidson to send me material on the school, and she kindly responded. By coincidence, my colleague (and wife) Pilar Soler and I had been asked to attend a conference sponsored by the European Community in Marseilles on Second Chance Schools, ones for students who had not succeeded in the past. Although we had reviewed the literature on high school dropouts and had formulated an Accelerated Schools approach to meeting the needs of those children, we had not been aware of any Accelerated Schools actually implementing the approach. Accordingly, when we received the material from Dr. Eidson, we were able to provide documentation for the application of the model in this context. Indeed, that paper was delivered by Soler in Marseilles in December 1996, and it was greeted with great enthusiasm by the Europeans, not only for its concepts, but for data on its application.

At this point, Eidson corresponded with us on her plan with Dr. Hillhouse to write a book on their project. I waited enthusiastically for their book and reviewed most of an early draft. My reading of the manuscript just increased my admiration for their accomplishments and their ability to apply the Accelerated Schools process and that of Caring Communities to adolescents, especially ones who had not experienced school success in the past. Thus, it is with great pleasure that I note the publication of their book for sharing with other educators who face similar challenges. It is an excellent presentation based on 3 years of "hands-on" experience, and it is a success story that is inspiring.

Within the context of the national Accelerated Schools Project, I have one important suggestion to guide the reader. The national Project attempts to transform schools by building skills within, providing tools to the school community, and offering a process that utilizes these tools and skills. As part of that transformation, schools must develop their own instruments and methods for the taking stock and vision stages, and they must also choose their own priorities. In addition, the authors use an inquiry or problem-solving process in order to understand the challenges that they face, their causes, and potential solutions.

Eidson and Hillhouse have chosen to generously share their own instruments and solutions from the Meramec Community School experience as illustrative. But, the Accelerated Schools Project is not a "cookie-cutter" approach to school reform. Even with the same tools and process, schools need to build on their own strengths, create their own living vision, develop their own instruments for taking stock, set out their own priorities, and apply the inquiry method uniquely to their challenges and their choice of, and implementation of, solutions. Although Eidson and Hillhouse have provided useful examples to buttress their presentation of the process that they followed, these should not be viewed as generic instruments or solutions. Instead, they are illustrative of how one particular community used these tools in a creative way to address its own unique challenges. Accelerated Schools require each school community to draw upon its own dreams, realities, and talents to apply the tools and process to its own situation.

Furthermore, Accelerated Schools require the guidance of a coach from the school community who is trained at our national center or one of our regional centers as well as continuing support from one of those centers. Information on training and support is readily available on our home page at http://www-leland.stanford.edu/group/ASU and in the many newsletters and publications of the Project, for example, Wendy Hopfenberg, Henry M. Levin, and Associates, *The Accelerated Schools Resource Guide* (San Francisco: Jossey-Bass, 1993) and Christine Finnan, Jane McCarthy, Edward St. John, and Simeon Slovacek (Eds.), *Accelerated Schools in Action: Lessons From the Field* (Thousand Oaks, CA: Corwin Press, 1995).

In no way should these concerns detract from the fine presentation and valuable accomplishments of the authors and the Meramec Valley Community School. Carrie Eidson and Edward Hillhouse have made an important contribution in combining Accelerated Schools and Caring Communities processes to create high schools that enable students to succeed. Their leadership has been of great value in moving these ideas forward into new settings, and the results speak for themselves. Most of all, they are not just theorists exhorting others to do it. They have done it themselves and deserve credit for both their understanding of the process and their putting it into practice.

HENRY M. LEVIN
Visiting Professor, Teachers College,
Columbia University (1997-1998)
and the David Jacks Professor of Higher
Education and Economics, Stanford University

Preface

Communities across America are demanding high school reform initiatives to ebb the rising current of students at risk of failing school and dropping out of school before graduating. Having students at risk for school failure is not a new phenomenon in American public high schools. Historically, these students have been in our schools for the past 300 years. The incidence of identified at-risk students is climbing at an alarming pace, however, as is the national dropout rate. There is a sharp rise in the number of students at risk of school failure who are experiencing depression, eating disorders, serious emotional disturbances, suicidal tendencies, drug and alcohol abuse, sexual abuse, apathy, and alienation as well as exhibiting violent, aggressive, and disruptive behavior in our schools today. Academic learning is not a priority in the lives of these teenagers.

High schools are witnessing an alarming increase in the number of young people dropping out of school before graduating and lacking the intellectual, emotional, and social skills necessary to be productive members of their community. According to a report by the National Association of Secondary School Principals (NASSP) and the Carnegie Foundation (1996), *Breaking Ranks: Changing an American Institution*, "A young person who grows into adulthood unequipped to reach his or her full potential will possess neither the knowledge nor the will to contribute to making this a better society" (p. 4). Our review of the literature and our personal observations indicate academic learning stops when students try to cope with social and emotional problems or issues stemming from their family or peers. Educators expect at-risk students to come to school every day, focus on specific academic tasks, be motivated to produce academically, and behave appropriately.

Educators, parents, legislators, and communities for national school reform initiatives have brought the issue of students at risk to the forefront. With the advent of Zero Tolerance laws, Safe School laws, Caring Communities programs, and the NASSP and Carnegie Foundation report, school districts and communities are facing the task of providing alternative education to serve and impact students with a history of school failure.

NOTE: The names of the students mentioned in this book are not real. The stories and case studies are a composite of students we have met and worked with through the years.

This book deals with school reform for students at risk of school failure. It is a book for the practicing administrator, teacher, counselor, social worker, college professor, prospective teacher, and anyone truly interested in preparing at-risk students to meet the challenges of our ever-changing society and become the future leaders, parents, and workforce in our society. As educators, we have the responsibility to work with the community to find effective ways to help at-risk students to become literate, problem-solving, productive, and responsible citizens in our communities.

The research and experience base for this book developed from our own need as educators in Pacific, Missouri, to address the high dropout rate of students in the Meramec Valley R-III School District. We undertook research to find the specific characteristics of the students who drop out in our district and compare them to students in schools across the nation. Research was also initiated to determine cultural and social issues that impact the academic success of these students. We found a limited number of books and articles that detail methods and instructional practices that work effectively with students at risk or advise on developing programs and schools that nurture these students. We looked for innovative methods and techniques that "turn on" at-risk teenagers to learning and staying in school to graduate. The Accelerated Schools philosophy combined with the Caring Communities philosophy proved to be the solution to motivating, nurturing, and challenging at-risk students to take responsibility for their learning process and future.

The chapters in this book result from our experiences as a superintendent of schools and principal of an Accelerated alternative high school for at-risk students and as adjunct professors at Southwest Baptist University, teaching courses on working with students at risk for school failure. Our firsthand experiences are coupled with studies of students at risk for school failure in the literature and site visits to other traditional and alternative middle and high schools around the country to give different perspectives and approaches. This book is intended to be a practical guide for understanding these students and the various educational, social, economic, and cultural issues that affect their success in school and in the community.

We examine the characteristics of students at risk and several solutions to break this cycle of dysfunction through effective instructional and behavioral techniques and practices. We discuss the success of the Accelerated Schools philosophy and Caring Communities philosophy with keeping at-risk students participating and achieving in an Accelerated high school. Successful strategies, practices, and alternative educational approaches are presented that may prove helpful to the readers in their classrooms and schools.

A detailed description on developing an Accelerated alternative high school, utilizing the Accelerated Schools philosophy in combination with the Caring Communities philosophy, is the thrust of this book. We developed the community school framework based on Dr. Henry Levin's Accelerated Schools philosophy (Hopfenberg, Levin, and Associates, 1993), which is very successful with getting at-risk students involved in their learning. This is an educational philosophy that finally makes sense for dealing with students and families with many problems. The Accelerated Schools philosophy is more humane and natural in its interaction with students at risk for school failure. We use case studies from our Community School throughout this book to illustrate concepts and discussions.

Chapter 1 discusses the plight of communities and schools, economically, physically, emotionally, and socially, when teenagers drop out of school before graduation. We examine the necessity for providing an Accelerated high school, an alternative school for at-risk students as a vehicle for decreasing the dropout rate and equipping these youth to become productive and responsible community members. The Accelerated Schools philosophy and its three principles are discussed with regard to creating a "dream school" for the staff, parents, and students in which consensus and collaboration from all school stakeholders are sought and encouraged.

The Accelerated Schools philosophy and Caring Communities philosophy, in combination, complement and easily mesh with the findings and recommendations in the NASSP and Carnegie Foundation (1996) report, *Breaking Ranks: Changing an American Institution*. This "meshing" is discussed in Chapter 2 with regard to building a caring school community. Other topics discussed in this chapter include reshaping the role of the principal, empowering the staff, empowering the students, and cultivating parent involvement.

Chapter 3 explains the Accelerated Schools process of *taking stock* of the strengths and weaknesses of the school to get baseline data of where the school is "right now." Some of the topics discussed are incorporating the three principles of the Accelerated Schools philosophy; forming the taking stock cadres; data collection activities; community, student, and parent taking stock and vision surveys; and data analysis.

Chapter 4 explains the importance of developing and implementing the *vision* that the stakeholders utilize in working together with a unity of purpose to create their dream school. Some of the topics discussed in Chapter 4 are the seeds of the living vision, creating the vision, branches of the living vision, Accelerated high school vision, the rationale, the philosophy, and educational theories and philosophies that work well with the Accelerated Schools philosophy and Caring Communities philosophy.

Chapter 5 discusses the *governance structure* needed to ensure the Accelerated Schools philosophy and Caring Communities philosophy are integrated correctly and the vision is achieved. The governance structure is the "keeper of the dream," continually keeping all the stakeholders focused and working with a unity of purpose, giving them empowerment with responsibility and building on their strengths.

Chapter 6 explores in detail the nuts and bolts of developing the actual Accelerated high school for at-risk students, from the student entrance criteria to the daily schedule. This chapter helps the reader fashion the skeleton, muscles, and heart of the Accelerated high school. It also discusses program evaluation and authentic assessment techniques for the program.

Chapter 7 explores effective techniques and strategies for working with at-risk students to help them become motivated and successful in the learning process. Social barriers and issues are discussed as they pertain to the blocking of academic progress in these students. The techniques given in this chapter are proven to be effective and powerful learning experiences as part of the instructional delivery system. The topics discussed include impact of social issues and barriers on learning, cognitive learning styles with regard to at-risk students, utilizing multiple intelligences theory, powerful learning experiences, Accelerated and challenging curriculum, developing the Accelerated curriculum, Constructivist theory, and instruction through technology.

Chapter 8 provides examples and discussions of the strategies that are effective in decreasing discipline problems through creating an environment of belonging, caring, responsibility, generosity, mastery, trust, respect, responsibility, and collaboration. Chapter 8 also discusses topics such as the student-teacher relationship, collaboration versus competition, and the impact of self-esteem on discipline problems.

The Resources section is complete with sample forms and surveys for readers to copy and use or adapt to their specific needs. We urge the readers to examine the specific needs of their students, parents, and community and use that data to develop forms and surveys that will give them information to develop an Accelerated high school that fits their needs. In addition to the References listing of works cited in the text, we include the Further Reading list of books and articles that may be useful for readers' further research.

This book is born out of a need to help our community fight the battle of keeping our young people in school and learning the necessary skills and information to become productive members of our community. Communities and schools lose socially, intellectually, physically, economically, and emotionally each time a teenager drops out of school. *The Accelerated High School: A Step-By-Step Guide for Administrators and Teachers* shows how communities and schools can design and develop their dream school to serve, nurture, and educate students at risk of school failure.

DR. CARRIE BAYLARD EIDSON
DR. EDWARD D. HILLHOUSE
Pacific, Missouri

Acknowledgments

Thank you, H. S., for your guidance and the patience and perseverance to see this project to the end.

Thank you to our families for giving us the time and space to think and write.

Thank you, Joan Solomon, for giving us the chance to become the first Accelerated high school, not only in Missouri but also in the nation.

A special thank you, Dr. Henry Levin, for your constant support and suggestions.

Thank you, Alice Foster, Acquisitions Editor, for believing in our book and always answering our many calls.

About the Authors

Dr. Carrie Baylard Eidson is Principal of the Meramec Valley Community School, an alternative school in Pacific, Missouri, for 8th through 12th graders who are at-risk students and Title I at-risk preschool children. In addition to her duties as the Community School Principal, she has been the Meramec Valley R-III Director of Special Services, which includes Director of at-risk students, Homeless Coordinator, Director of Titles I and VI, Special Education, and 504 Coordinator for the last 12 years. She has experience as a social worker, counselor, regular education and special education teacher, psychological examiner, and principal with regard to working with at-risk children and youth. She is an Adjunct Professor at Southwest Baptist University, developing and teaching graduate-level courses on developing an Accelerated High School, alternative education programs and effective practices for working with the at-risk. Dr. Eidson is also an Adjunct Professor at the Missouri Institute of Mental Health, a Center for University of Missouri-Columbia, developing and implementing research programs for building resiliency in at-risk youth utilizing the Accelerated Schools Philosophy, the Caring Community Philosophy, and Community Service Learning.

Dr. Edward D. Hillhouse is Superintendent of Schools for the Meramec Valley R-III School District in Pacific, Missouri. The Community School for students at risk was his brainchild. He saw the need for addressing identified at-risk students and, working with Dr. Carrie Eidson as principal of the school, established a program that has achieved a high degree of success. He also has served as a classroom teacher, assistant principal, principal, assistant superintendent, and adjunct professor in both masters program in education and advanced programs in administration. As superintendent, he successfully coordinated efforts to pass bond issues and tax levies, and he established the first public school preschool in the area. Improving the climate of respect between teachers, administrations, and students through proactive approaches such as the Accelerated high school is an example of such success. He has served as presdient of the South Central Missouri Association of School Administrators, as president of the Pacific Area Chamber of Commerce, and as the leader for a Missouri School Improvement program.

Coming Together

We all came from one place,
But still, nobody wanted to
accept us. . . .
We understood each other and
Accepted everybody's differences.
Yet we were still pushed away.
We came to this school and
Instead of being many,
We became one.

HATTIE SMITH
Senior class, 1996
Meramec Valley Community School

1

When Communities
Lose the Battle in Schools

"America is not like a blanket—one piece of cloth,
the same color, the same texture, the same size. America
is more like a quilt—many colors, many sizes, all woven
and held together by a common thread."

Jesse Jackson
(Fitzhenry, 1993, p. 14)

As communities sit before the television watching the evening news night after night, they are bombarded with stories concerning the battle our communities are losing in our schools because of high dropout rates, violence, alienation, and apathetic teenagers in traditional high schools today. It is common to find lead stories with scenarios such as the following:

The evening news anchorman looks seriously into the camera, informing millions of television viewers that a 15-year-old boy walked into his crowded classroom this morning and fatally shot four students and his teacher. The boy with the gun was angry because his classmates teased him unmercifully about being retained three times. The young teenager felt his teacher did not care enough to make his classmates stop hurting him.

The police chief is baffled by the rise in juvenile crime and gang-related activities that have invaded his suburban community in the last few years. He does not have enough police officers to interdict the easy availability of drugs, alcohol, and guns circulating among the teenagers and young adults in the community. The chief talks about the affluence of this community making it easy for the teenagers to buy the drugs and guns. He tells the reporter that his staff sees more and more teenagers just "hanging out" on the streets both day and night, acting as if they have no desire to "make something out of themselves."

The chief wonders aloud why the schools are not doing more to keep young people in school and teach them "something useful. . . . After all, they will be running this community someday." The police chief stares at the scene in front of the school. He sadly shakes his head and gets into the police car with the young murderer.

The remote control button is pressed and the channel changes:

A newswoman walks through the hallways of a run-down high school building, housing a large minority student population. She asks the principal why the student test scores have been decreasing over the past 5 years while the student dropout rate has been increasing. The principal informs the reporter that his school consists of a student population with 80% of the students eligible for free or reduced-fee lunches and living below the poverty level. He asks the reporter how the community expects these teenagers to care about learning when their basic human needs are not being met.

The third station shows a reporter standing in front of a rural high school:

The reporter tells the viewers that businesses in this small community are disappointed with the low academic skill levels of entry-level workers today. With rising high school dropout rates, communities are faced with an increasing population of young, unskilled, and unemployed workers. It is very hard for rural, suburban, or urban communities to attract new businesses when the labor force is unskilled. To combat the loss of the present and future labor force, many businesses have implemented academic and work training programs for unskilled workers. The cost of training these dropouts continues to rise, which in turn results in a loss of economic productivity for businesses and communities.

As the nation listened to the 1997 State of the Union address, President Bill Clinton spoke of making school reform a priority by decreasing the country's large and increasing dropout rate while producing literate and socially responsible citizens. The president emphasized building "caring communities" to ensure that all Americans have adequate food, clothing, health services, housing, and a safe neighborhood in which to live. He urged communities to adopt the African Proverb, "It takes a whole village to raise a child," to improve the quality of life for America's people while bringing peace and prosperity to our communities.

In the 1990s, U.S. high schools are witnessing an increasing population of young, undereducated, poorly trained teenagers dropping out of school before graduating. The price we are paying for our ever-increasing at-risk population cannot just be measured in economic terms. The high rate of students leaving high school before graduation threatens the social, intellectual, cultural, moral, physical, and emotional health of our communities (Clifford, 1990).

Our American heritage and societal values are endangered with the increase of our at-risk population. These children and teenagers must be able to read and demonstrate reasoning skills in order to understand our society's mores and culture. Our democracy depends on having citizens who can interpret information and make sound judgments concerning our government institutions, finances, and business dealings.

The Battle in Our Schools to Educate At-Risk Students

For the past decade, communities throughout our nation have continued to lose the battle of successfully educating *all* children in our schools. According to McWhirter, McWhirter, McWhirter, and McWhirter (1993) and Capuzzi and Gross (1996), barriers to winning the battles include the following:

- 700,000 teenagers per year leave high school before graduating.
- 500,000 robberies, burglaries, rapes, and assaults are committed in schools each year.
- 3 million students and teachers are victims of crime each year.
- 7,000 teenagers commit suicide each year.
- 24 million children live in poverty.
- 500,000 teenagers give birth each year. (Capuzzi & Gross, 1996, p. 5)

According to Carolyn Warner (1997), each day in America

- 100,000 children are homeless.
- 8,400 children are reported abused or neglected.
- 135,000 children take guns to school. (p. 32)

These children are at risk for school failure and run a high risk of dropping out before graduating from high school.

The Meramec Valley Community Battle

By 1992, Pacific, Missouri, the rural community of 25,000 people in which the two of us live was losing the battle in its high school. Juvenile crime was up 31% over the year before; 49% of our student population lived in single-parent families and 51% lived in households with two adults, married or otherwise. Twenty percent of our students received Medicaid and 45% received free or reduced-fee lunches; 31% of the children in our community lived in poverty, and 15% of our school district population received special education services. The school district has experienced a growth of 100 to 200 new students in grades 1 through 12 each year since 1992. It is located directly outside of Saint Louis County, and the metropolitan population is moving west to our community.

The socioeconomic makeup of our community is low to upper-middle class and can be classified as heavily transient. The transient nature of the community consists not only of great movement in and out of the district but also of movement within the district boundaries. The economic composition of the community includes farmers, blue-collar workers, small family-owned businesses, and a minority of white collar or professional workers.

During the 1995-1996 school year, our school district had 92 homeless children, most of whom were 14 to 18 years old. Teenage pregnancies had risen 10% over the past 5 years. The end-of-the-year police report indicated that juvenile crime had started to rise again in 1996 after tapering off for 2 years. The police interviewed attribute the increase to the growing population and gang activity moving to Pacific. Due to the large number of single-parent families, blended families, stepfamilies, and grandparents as heads of households, along with an increase in teenage pregnancy, homelessness, juvenile crime, and the high school dropout rate, it can be said the Meramec Valley R-III School District has a large at-risk student population.

According to the large number of referrals to the middle school and high school offices, many of those identified as at-risk students seek violent, aggressive, or disruptive solutions to problems they encounter at school. Many other identified at-risk students simply "fade out" and quietly leave school because of feelings of alienation, frustration, or apathy. These findings agree with those in the literature

(Barber, & McCellen, 1987; Brendtro, Brokenleg, & Van Bockern, 1990). Counselors at our district schools report that these students need extra assistance in academic skills, social skills, self-esteem, self-responsibility, and motivation.

One problem we found is that at-risk students and their parents often do not view education as a priority in their lives. The parents of these children are fighting for emotional and financial survival themselves and have little energy or time to become involved with their child's education. Many of these parents were at-risk students themselves and have bad memories of their years in schools. They tend to mistrust or show apathy toward schools today.

Our community fought an economic, physical, and social battle as more and more at-risk families moved into the community. The board of education requested that the two of us, as Superintendent (Dr. Edward Hillhouse) and Director of Special Services (Dr. Carrie Eidson), research the impact of high school dropouts on other communities and school districts. Through our review of the literature; interviews with educators, students, parents, community members, and State Department of Education administrators; and site visits to other schools, we found that communities everywhere are negatively affected when students drop out of high school before graduating. We found we were not alone in the battle to reclaim our community and awaken at-risk teenagers to the life changes an education can make.

In *Savage Inequalities* (1991), Jonathan Kozol writes about his observations of the devastating effects on a community when its school system does not produce literate and skilled young people for its labor force. He tells of communities in Chicago and Cincinnati in which family celebrations occur when their children graduate from eighth grade because few stay in school to graduate from high school. This has been occurring in the 1990s throughout our country!

How academically and socially prepared is an eighth-grade child to join the community's labor force and help the community's economic productivity level rise? How can an eighth-grade education allow that child to earn enough money to eventually support a family, buy a home, or provide for his or her retirement? Chances are high that semi-educated children will eventually become a burden to their families and communities by experiencing such things as

- Teenage pregnancy
- Drug or alcohol abuse
- Jail time for criminal activities
- Inability to support themselves without government assistance
- Homelessness

Kozol (1991) gives pointed descriptions of communities and schools in East Saint Louis, Illinois; New York; and New Jersey in which teachers and students have outdated textbooks, poor facilities, and little or no supplies or materials to properly educate young people for today's society. He speaks of the hopelessness and despair on children's faces. These children are highly at risk for school failure. The situation becomes a vicious cycle producing generation after generation of unskilled, uneducated, and unmotivated young people who cannot effectively contribute to the well-being and improvement of their communities.

School districts in Delaware, Iowa, Kansas, and Montana, for example, have seen a rise in their at-risk student populations through an increase in

- Single-parent families
- The need for more social services to keep families together
- Students on free or reduced-fee lunches
- Identified at-risk student population
- Dropout rate
- Emancipated high school students
- Homeless children
- Non-English-speaking immigrant students (Warner, 1997)

Through interviews with teachers and administrators in and outside our school district and through a review of the literature, we see and hear that educators are less handicapped in teaching their subject matter than in addressing the problems students bring to the classroom. The consensus we find among teachers and administrators is that schools are being bombarded by social issues and problems such as teen pregnancy, teen suicide, violence, depression, and family dysfunction, which interferes with the learning process and academic and social progress of students. We find these problems exist in all communities: urban, suburban, and rural.

Studies indicate these social issues and problems contribute to the cause of students becoming at risk for school failure or dropping out (Capuzzi & Gross, 1996). This shows that any student, regardless of socioeconomic status or race, is vulnerable to becoming labeled "at risk" at any stage of his or her educational career. Students can move in and out of at-risk situations, producing gaps in their learning that lead to frustration with school.

What Makes Teenagers Leave School?

Educators need to recognize the social issues and problems that influence school achievement and motivation for learning. Schools need to develop prevention and crisis plans to stop this cause of school failure. Educators must also be aware these problems are manifested in the following ways:

- Tardiness
- Truancy
- Poor grades
- Behavior problems in school and in the community
- Violence
- Problems with authority figures
- Depression
- Drug and alcohol abuse
- Retention in one or more grades
- Teen suicide
- Eating disorders
- Teenage pregnancy

According to Ekstrom, Goertz, Pollack, and Rock (1986), the following factors are major determinants of why students drop out of school:

- Inability to tolerate structured activities and strict schedules
- Behavior problems
- Low grades

- Family circumstances
- Few, if any, significant adult supports for their educational progress
- Parents uninvolved with students' schooling
- Friends with similar attitudes and problems concerning school
- Alienation at large traditional schools

We, the authors, have found other factors for dropping out of school through our interviews with students who have left school before graduating:

- Students assumed financial responsibilities for their nuclear family and needed to obtain full-time employment.
- Students were stigmatized by labels of negative categories and left school to salvage self-pride and dignity.
- Students were bored with a traditional passive learning instructional delivery system.
- Students did not find the curriculum challenging.
- Students felt they had little or no choice or control over their learning process.
- Students did not have a sense of belonging to the traditional school.
- Students saw no connection between learned academic information and the "real world."

These students tend to fade into the woodwork if they do not have a significant adult at school with whom to connect. Research shows that students who do not have regular and meaningful contact with teachers never really become assimilated into the school community (Wehlage, Rutter, & Turnbaugh, 1987).

Community School Student Self-Esteem Survey

Of the 105 students at the Community School, an Accelerated high school in Pacific, Missouri, 93% indicated through a student survey that they felt alienated and unnoticed at their traditional high schools. On the Self-Esteem Index (SEI) survey, 90% of the students scored in the low range for self-perceived academic confidence and self-esteem on the initial testing before entering the Community School. Our findings agree with Wehlage et al.'s (1987) study in which the researchers found that both students who are labeled "at risk" and those who have dropped out have very poor self-esteem. These students indicate they feel many of their teachers throughout their school careers have had very little interest in them and did not treat them as worthwhile individuals.

Many of the students we have interviewed blame large class sizes and a large total student body as contributing to their feelings of alienation and disconnectedness. They complain about walking down the crowded hallways, lunch lines that never end, and having to travel from one end of the building to the next for classes. They indicate they are always put in the classes for "slow learners" or "vocational education" instead of the college-bound track. These students are angry because no one at their past schools asked them what they wanted or guided them toward the college-bound curriculum.

When asked what clubs or extracurricular activities they participated in at the traditional school, 95% said none. Reasons cited for nonparticipation include the following:

- "Only prep kids got to do anything important at school."
- "I have to work after school and can't hang around for clubs."

- "No teacher asked me to join their club like I saw them ask other kids."
- "I didn't feel comfortable around the kids who were in the clubs."
- "The coaches didn't like me in their PE classes so I didn't make the school football team."

We must understand these teenagers do not view school as a priority in their lives. They do not see that getting an education can help them change some of the negative aspects of their lives.

- Have we as professional educators failed to show them the connection?
- Have we as educators somehow shown our students that we are only interested in test scores and not in the students as unique, worthwhile individuals?
- Have we inadvertently planted the seeds of student alienation and apathy through our failure to understand their life circumstances?

The structure of our large traditional schools diminishes the opportunities for students to become friends with their teachers. The school-student relationship has become bogged down in impersonal nods and small talk. Students and teachers do not relate to one another as real, whole persons, but in segments of 50-minute periods with prescribed roles (Brendtro et al., 1990). Research indicates that too often teachers feel pressured to complete a textbook or a set of objectives by the end of the school year. Teacher accountability based on student achievement test scores is another added pressure on the teacher to cram as much information as possible into a 50-minute period. This leaves little, if any, time for the development of strong bonds between teachers and students.

Teachers and students do not seem to "hang around" after school as they did in the 1940s, 1950s, and 1960s, because most students currently are transported to and from school by buses. The days of the old neighborhood school within walking distance from home are all but gone. Now students must rush to catch the bus home, which may be a 40- to 50-minute ride from school. Because of the transportation issue, there is no longer time for students to have informal chats with teachers after school and begin to develop relationships.

The pressures of student and teacher alienation always slow the learning process. Alienation breeds apathy on the part of both the student and the teacher. At-risk students in particular see themselves on the "other side of the fence" from other students and from the teachers. In turn, they lose motivation and eventually drop out because they feel they cannot get along in specific schools (Deblois, 1989). Most studies show that student alienation begins as early as kindergarten. By the time these students reach middle school, alienation and apathy are well ingrained (Madden & Slavin, 1989). Too often, our schools have failed to provide at-risk students proper counseling, diverse instructional techniques, and behavior incentives that could end their feelings of alienation (Ralph, 1989). But schools do not have to continue on this path of failure and lose large numbers of young people before graduation each year.

Schools today are not equipped to deal with the social conflicts that youth bring with them. Schools are not providing a supportive environment (Waxman, Walker de Felix, Anderson, & Baptiste, 1992). We as educators should recognize that schools do not and cannot exist in a vacuum. Schools need to work collaboratively with parents, students, and the community to address the issues affecting school success for these children.

Can Communities Win
the Battle in Our Schools?

For decades, schools have existed as complete entities of their own, in total isolation from their surrounding community. The result has been a complete separation of schools and communities, each working with its own goals and visions. As the 1990s began, schools and communities found themselves sharing an increasing number of problems.

Schools and communities are slowly beginning to understand they need each other to achieve their goals and visions. A small but increasing number of schools and communities are sharing the same goals and visions for producing responsible, educated, and productive citizens through *school-community partnerships*. They are combining their talents and resources while developing new relationships and school reforms to keep at-risk students in school through graduation (Eidson & Hillhouse, 1997).

Governor Mel Carnahan of Missouri and Governor Jim Edgars of Illinois, among other state governors, have passed school reform initiatives attempting to decrease the dropout rate by making education interesting, motivating, and relevant to students' lives. The U.S. Department of Education's Goals 2000 initiative, the Caring Communities philosophy, Safe Schools acts, Zero Tolerance laws, and Accelerated Schools projects are some of the school reform initiatives developed to keep our schools safe from violence and to address the educational, social, and emotional needs of an ever-growing population of students at risk for school failure.

School reform initiatives are guides or mandates to promote change from within the school. To make effective changes in their schools, however, educators must take a deep, hard look at

- The characteristics of their specific at-risk student population
- The life situations of their at-risk students
- The values, needs, and culture of the community at large
- The culture, values, and needs of the school community
- Alternative education techniques and programs that motivate at-risk students to stay in school
- The aspects of the traditional high school that "turn off" at-risk students
- The reasons why students drop out of school
- The effects on the larger community of students dropping out

We have found in our experiences dealing with students at risk for school failure that we need to be careful not to view these students as the problem but rather to examine the outside factors that place them in at-risk situations or circumstances. The social issues, life circumstances, and educational culture are the core forces that create an environment putting these students at risk for school failure.

Communities can win the battle in schools if they work collaboratively with schools to meet the specific needs of students at risk for school failure and their families. Schools and communities that work together become more people oriented and caring over time. They work together to make their "dream school" where the curriculum, atmosphere, and culture reflect the values, needs, and culture of the community.

Schools must show students the relevancy and connection between education and real-life situations. Schools must become "Caring Communities" in which every student feels a sense of belonging, acceptance, and success. Schools must find ways to keep students actively participating, motivated, and interested in learning for learning's sake. They must find ways to erase the student alienation and feelings of apathy that are the main reasons teenagers leave school.

The Solution

After researching and visiting other schools and communities, we were convinced traditional prevention and intervention strategies of remediation, labeling, watering down curriculum, passive learning activities, memorizing textbook facts, and filling out worksheets did not meet the intellectual, social, emotional, and physical needs of at-risk students. With the help of our community planning team, we developed and proposed a school in which at-risk students would feel accepted and possess a sense of belonging. We proposed

- A caring, family-like environment
- Academic acceleration
- Hands-on individual projects
- Community service learning projects
- Student-centered and student-driven curriculum
- Collaboration between staff, students, parents, and the community in every aspect of the school's programs and procedures
- Active learning experiences and participatory instruction
- Technology as a major focus of the instructional delivery system
- Informal physical setting
- Student responsibility and control in learning process
- Wraparound services for the students and their families to help break the cycle of family dysfunction so our students stay in school to receive a high school diploma

In August 1994, the Meramec Valley Community School opened its doors to 105 8th- through 12th-grade students who were identified as being at risk for school failure. This school is designed in response to Goals 2000 and the Missouri State Department of Elementary and Secondary Education's response to that initiative, the Missourians' Prepared Goal of immediate action needed for all youth who are in danger of failing or leaving school. We purposefully designed the Community School's program so that it could easily be replicated by other high schools. This program can be integrated into large high schools as well as small high schools or alternative high schools. We have a yearly enrollment of 105 to 115 at-risk students in grades 8 through 12.

The foundation of our school is Dr. Henry M. Levin's Accelerated Schools philosophy in combination with the Caring Communities philosophy. The school is closely aligned with the findings in the NASSP and Carnegie Foundation (1996) report *Breaking Ranks: Changing an American Institution*. This school fills a need by providing a setting that is deliberately differentiated from the traditional middle school and high school. It is structured for greater flexibility, family-like atmosphere, active student participation, powerful learning experiences, and close family involvement to bring about the increased desire on the student's part to stay in school and graduate.

The Community School's total student population is made up of teenagers at risk of school failure. The teenagers who apply for and are accepted into the Community school are "street wise." They have problems with authority figures and drugs and alcohol and often display violent, aggressive, or disruptive behavior. Most have experienced sexual abuse, depression, or eating disorders. They have above-average intelligence, many in the gifted range. These young people felt alienated and "outside the circle" as students in the traditional high school. They showed little if any motivation or initiative to participate in class activities, discussions, or assignments. The majority of the Community School students came to our school with histories of attendance problems, truancies, out-of-school suspensions, in-school suspensions, and retentions. Ninety of the 115 students presently at the Community School are eligible for Title I services because of their low reading levels. Their low reading levels are due to huge gaps in reading skills because of the large amount of time absent from school throughout their years of education. All of our students were very unmotivated to learn, and graduating from high school was not a priority when they came to the entrance interview with the Community School staff.

Utilizing the Accelerated Schools philosophy and the Caring Communities philosophy as the foundation of our school has yielded such results as

- There is a dropout rate of only 2%.
- 95% of students in grades 9 to 12 earn an average of seven credits per school year.
- Attendance has increased by 10% each year since the school's opening in August 1994. At the end of the 1996-1997 school year, it was at 89%.
- 65% of our graduating seniors over the past 3 years attend junior colleges, 10% are in the military, 10% are working full-time, 10% attend vocational technical schools, 4% are doing nothing, and 1% attend a 4-year college.
- Parent involvement increased by 10% each year as compared to the same parents' involvement when their children attended the traditional school. Comparisons are made through attendance sheets from parent topic meetings, events, parent-teacher conferences, and cadre work.
- Out-of-school suspensions for students attending the Community School have decreased by 15% as compared to the same students' records when they attended the traditional high school.
- 90% of students taking a pre and post Self-Esteem Index (SEI) survey displayed a 3-point increase in their own perception of their academic ability confidence level on the end-of-the-year posttest. A 3-point increase was our goal as these students had very negative attitudes and perceptions with regard to their personal academic abilities. After an academically and socially successful school year, 90% of our students felt more confident about their academic abilities.
- The Community School has a 35- to 40-student waiting list.

Many of our at-risk students and their parents view school as composed of unrelated bits and pieces of knowledge. They do not see the connection between information learned in school and real-life situations. Reading and memorizing chapters in textbooks, taking notes in lecture classes, and answering multiple choice tests "turn off" at-risk students. Through the "meshing" of the Accelerated Schools philosophy and the Caring Communities philosophy, at-risk students become motivated, awakened, active participants in an interactive school environment. We see students utilizing the inquiry process to solve problems and organize projects as they work toward achieving the three principles of the Accelerated

Schools process: unity of purpose, empowerment with responsibility, and building on strengths.

The Accelerated Schools philosophy focuses on the belief that *all* children can learn if presented with an accelerated and challenging curriculum. It also advocates treating each child as if he or she is gifted and talented. This philosophy is a belief system that requires the collaboration of students, staff, parents, and the community to create their dream school, a school they would want their children to attend (Hopfenberg et al., 1993). Accelerated Schools have the following components:

- High expectations for all students
- Clear vision and goals to make students academic achievers
- Concepts and skills taught through powerful learning experiences based on stimulating problem solving
- Application of learned academic information to relevant real-life situations
- Building on the strengths of students, staff, and parents
- Practicing collaboration and consensus among staff, students, and parents in all aspects of the Accelerated school

The Accelerated Schools process, when integrated throughout the curriculum, brings the classroom out into the community. This enables the students and staff to find solutions to challenging problems while connecting academic information to real-life situations. The Accelerated high school has built its foundation on three principles:

- Unity of purpose
- Empowerment with responsibility
- Building on strengths

Chapter Summary

In this chapter, we have seen that American education is at a crucial crossroad. Dropout rates, welfare rolls, child and adult crime, child abuse, and teenage drug use are increasing at an alarming rate, negatively affecting families, schools, and communities socially, emotionally, physically, intellectually, and economically. It is time that educators take a hard look at our educational system and find solutions to student alienation and failure for learning. Schools and communities need to make *all* children feel worthwhile, successful, and welcome.

Is it possible for all schools to become "safe homes" for our students and parents? Is it possible all students can feel welcomed and important so they opt to participate instead of "fading into the woodwork"? Is it possible for our schools to be a place where all students are "inside the circle"? It not only can happen, but it is happening throughout the country with programs being initiated for students at risk for school failure.

Through the integration of the Accelerated Schools philosophy, Caring Communities philosophy, and the recommendations from the NASSP and Carnegie Foundation (1996) report *Breaking Ranks*, communities can win the battle in schools. Schools and communities that work together become more people oriented and caring over time. Schools change to reflect the values, needs, and issues affecting their community. Schools develop curriculums that incorporate academics and apply learned information to real-life situations in their community.

Students are taught they have a responsibility to their families, friends, and community to become involved in improving the community in which they live. Students develop personal meaning and understanding of the workings of their community as they find their "place" in it (Eidson & Hillhouse, 1997).

As we look across our nation, we find Accelerated elementary and middle schools developing very innovative methods and programs in dealing with *all* children. In Accelerated schools, the labels and stigmas disappear and real learning takes place. The seeds of self-esteem and academic confidence are nurtured and guided by caring and involved teachers and administrators. In these schools, it is being shown that parents, students, and staffs can build firm bonds and commitments to each other.

Accelerated high schools can be just such schools to help communities win the battle to decrease high school dropout rates while helping teenagers find a sense of belonging and acceptance.

2

Building a Caring
School Community

"They shall mount up with wings like eagles,
They shall run and not be weary,
They shall walk and not be faint."

Isaiah 40:31
(New International Version)

The eagle is a good analogy for the Accelerated high school's expectations for what it wants its students to become. The teenagers of today will impact our community as adults in a few years. Our schools have the responsibility of educating students to be literate, productive, and responsible citizens. We want our students to be effective and successful school and community leaders who possess character traits of the eagle such as

- Eagles fly alone and do not follow the flock because of peer pressure or personal insecurity.
- Eagles are committed to their goals and mission.
- Eagles soar above life's storms, never getting tossed about or blown off the path they have chosen.
- Eagles are committed to their mates and children, always providing for their needs. They are also caring and nurturing to others.
- Eagles are problem solvers, always looking for fresh ideas and solutions.
- Eagles are patient and have learned to wait for personal gratification.
- Eagles never look back or down; rather they always look ahead, keeping their mission in view.
- Eagles always make their homes on high rocks that are solidly grounded. Human leaders build their lives on their talents and strengths, creating a solid foundation.
- Eagles teach their children to be independent, committed, motivated, and curious to learn and soar with knowledge.

The majority of America's high schools do not produce very many eagles among their student populations. At-risk teenagers, like eagles, need a caring and nurturing environment in which risk taking, problem solving, a sense of belonging, social and personal responsibility, generosity, learning, and student empowerment are fostered and encouraged. To help young people soar like eagles, educators need to develop school communities in which students feel competent, useful, and in control of their learning process. All students can benefit from participating in a caring school community, but at-risk students desperately need a true environment of belonging and acceptance to become resilient and optimistic instead of alienated, apathetic, and useless (Sagor, 1996).

According to the NASSP and Carnegie Foundation (1996) report *Breaking Ranks: Changing an American Institution,* high schools must become caring communities in which parents, staff, students, and the community at large work collaboratively to make the school environment one in which students find a sense of belonging, satisfaction, and fulfillment. The Accelerated high school is a caring community in which at-risk students can reach their full potential by staying in school and graduating. It embodies the following recommendations of the *Breaking Ranks* report:

- Integrate essential knowledge in the curriculum and connect it to real-life situations
- Engage students in their own learning through active, participatory instructional strategies
- Create a school environment and climate conducive to teaching and learning
- Use technology as an instructional tool
- Provide flexible education through restructuring space and time
- Provide authentic assessment of individual, collective, and institutional outcomes and accountability
- Provide professional development to fulfill staff potential
- Find strength in diversity among staff, students, and parents
- Streamline the governance and operation of the high school and school district using more site-based management styles
- Make decisions regarding budget and staff allocations at the site level
- Nurture and support leadership of the principal, staff, students, parents, and others in the community to achieve the vision of the school
- Form school-community partnerships to coordinate the delivery of health and social services for students
- Form a web of support and collaboration with colleges and universities in the restructuring process

What Is a *Caring Community?*

In a *Caring Community,* people help people in, for example, the following ways:

- Checking on elderly shut-ins to make sure they are well and have food, heat, clothing, and companionship
- Making sure the homeless have shelters to go to or helping them find permanent housing
- Volunteering to help in the schools as clerical aides, readers for children, playground supervisors, etc.
- Securing jobs or job training for the unemployed
- Providing medical services for families and children
- Feeding the community hungry
- Transporting people to doctor appointments, jobs, etc.
- Teaching parenting skills to break the cycle of abuse and family dysfunction
- Providing emotional support for community members in crisis
- Providing counseling for adults, teenagers, and children in crisis
- Providing recreational activities for community members of all ages
- Extending friendship and support from neighbor to neighbor

A Caring Community fosters a sense of belonging and acceptance in its members. It cherishes and nurtures the talents and strengths of the individuals who live within its boundaries. It makes everyone feel needed, important, and worthwhile. A Caring Community supports its schools financially, physically, and emotionally. In a Caring Community, the school and community share the same vision and goals.

Building a Caring Community involves establishing a school-community partnership to collaborate and reach consensus to solve problems or provide new opportunities for individual and community growth. The school is usually the initiator and focal point of a Caring Community, since it comes in contact with the majority of the community families and children each day.

The major goal of a Caring Community is to provide wraparound services to families in crisis or continuous dysfunction to

- Help break generational cycles of family dysfunction
- Help stabilize families through various services and agencies
- Help children remain successfully in school and earn a high school diploma
- Help children remain in their own home, avoiding out-of-home placement in foster care or residential group home facilities and hospitalization for emotional and social problems
- Help children avoid becoming part of the juvenile justice system
- Help children learn how to make good, healthy, safe, life choices and decisions as well as acquire coping skills for life pressures and situations
- Work with students' crisis support counselor, parents, and siblings to enable the family as a whole to become functional, stable, and independent
- Increase students' attendance rates and decrease truancy rates
- Decrease the overall high school dropout rate
- Develop an intact value system in students
- Decrease violent, aggressive, and disruptive student outbursts in the school setting and the community setting
- Decrease out-of-school suspensions, in-school suspensions, and expulsions
- Develop a sense of belonging, acceptance, positive self-esteem, and personal responsibility in students with regard to self, the school, and the community
- Develop webs of school and community support services for the families of at-risk students to increase parenting skills, coping skills, family stability, and emotional support so families can help their children stay in school, achieve academically and socially, and graduate from high school
- Help students develop strong bonds with significant adults within the school and the community as a support system
- Decrease depression, eating disorders, suicidal feelings, and other mental illnesses in students that prevent academic learning to progress
- Decrease drug and alcohol abuse
- Decrease juvenile delinquent behavior problems in the school and the community

The Caring Community Family Substation

One way to provide unduplicated wraparound services entails the creation of the *Caring Community Family Substation*, which is housed within the Accelerated high school. The Family Substation provides a web of mental health, medical, dental, and social support services to help at-risk students acquire coping skills, emotional stability, and social skills necessary to obtain successful academic achievement and remain in school through graduation. This web of support services also extends to the families of the at-risk students to develop stability, emotional support, and a nurturing home environment for the entire family.

The goal of the Family Substation is to provide the wraparound services discussed on preceding pages to at-risk students and their families to enable and empower them as a whole to become functional, stable, supportive, nurturing, and independent family units in order for at-risk students to remain in school and graduate as productive community members. The Family Substation is designed to bring mental health services into the community and school for at-risk youth and their families while also providing other wraparound support services to aid in the stabilization of families and decrease of family dysfunction. The following wraparound mental health, medical, and social services can be provided by purchasing services from a mental health consortium:

Youth and Family Wraparound Services

- Crisis counseling at the high school and in the home
- Intensive family therapy in the home setting
- Individual and group counseling for students for drug and alcohol abuse; serious emotional disturbance; sexual, physical, and emotional abuse; eating disorders; depression; and other areas of concern
- 24-hour teen and parent crisis hotline service and mobile emergency outreach for immediate access to crisis situations in the community that require face-to-face counselor assessment or crisis intervention for possible immediate hospitalization
- Emergency placement program for homeless or abused teens
- Vocational rehabilitation counseling for employment and other support services for disabled youth and adults
- Employment counseling for nondisabled youth and adults with access via computer links to the Department of Labor's Employment Search Service.
- Taking Medicaid applications and arranging for client interviews with Division of Family Services caseworker to determine eligibility
- Referral services and setting up appointments for client medical and dental needs
- Psychological evaluations for children, youth, and adults, with follow-up counseling if needed
- Referral services for infant and child care for teenage parents to enable the teens to stay in school and graduate
- Collaboration with community homeless shelter, food pantry, and other agencies to help obtain needed basics of food, shelter, and clothing
- Collaboration with school staff to develop action plans for at-risk students and families to allow these students to remain in school
- Collaboration with state and local agencies to help at-risk students and families become stable and independent

The Caring Community Family Substation is a collaborative partnership between a school district and the consortium of mental health service providers. The Caring Community Family Substation is different from other youth and family mental health collaborative partnerships such as the Youth Service centers in Kentucky. The Kentucky model is designed and implemented as a referral service center only, with direct services given at the center.

In the Caring Community Family Substation model, the student and family mental health and other support services are given directly in the substation, which is located in a specific location in the Accelerated high school. This allows for immediate access for crisis counseling for students at the school when the students need to be removed from the classroom or campus. Having the substation located in the school allows for easy access for counseling with parents and the rest of the family in their home without losing precious time to traveling great distances. It also allows the mental health team at the substation to become familiar with the community and school values, beliefs, attitudes, and needs. The wraparound services listed previously are conducted by the substation staff in the high school.

The Caring Community Family Substation needs to be open to the students, school staff, and community Monday through Friday from 7 a.m. until 9 p.m. throughout the year. Crisis support counselors will be housed at the substation to cover drop-in students and parents and crisis situations that occur during the school day, conduct individual and group therapy, conduct home therapy and family assessments, and conduct psychological evaluations if necessary.

Crisis support counselors are responsible for the 24-hour teen and parent crisis hotline and mobile emergency outreach. Counselors also secure emergency shelter for abused, homeless, or runaway teenagers while working with the family for the goal of reunification if possible.

Students and families can be referred to the Caring Community Family Substation in the following ways:

- Student or family self-referral
- Parent referral of child
- Parent referral for personal therapy
- Referral by teachers, administrators, school counselors, or school nurses
- Referral by doctors or hospitals
- Referral through the juvenile court system
- Referral by the Division of Family Services
- Referral by the Division of Youth Services
- Referral by the Division of Mental Health
- Referral by homeless shelters
- Referral by other social agencies or organizations
- Referral by individual community members

The rationale for the Caring Community Family Substation is that at-risk students and their families are less likely to feel threatened by the offer of needed mental health and other support services if the services are linked with and housed in the high school. The school is often viewed as the focal point of the community, and parents are used to attending academic, sports, and fine arts events there. The school location brings the mental health services to the students at school and the families in their home setting without the families having to travel to another community for these services, as often is the case in rural communities. By housing the Caring Community Family Substation in the Accelerated high school, the parents and students become familiar with its purpose and services and look on it as a part of the school.

In a Caring Community, the community opens itself up to the school as it becomes a partner in educating and providing wraparound services for at-risk students and their families. Community members such as retired senior citizens, staff of social agencies and organizations, police officers, businesspeople, city officials, and church leaders are invited and welcomed to spend time in the school, interacting and planning with the administration, staff, students, and parents. A

Caring School Community fosters the creation of a Caring Community outside of the school building to help its students stay in school and graduate.

Fostering a Caring School Community

The Accelerated high school is a Caring School Community in which staff, student, and parent participation, collaboration, and engagement are sought, encouraged, and nurtured. Its main focus is to help at-risk students become like eagles—strong leaders and independent, caring, nurturing, goal-centered, responsible persons motivated to continue to learn past high school graduation. According to Wehlage, Rutter, Smith, Lesko, and Fernandez (1989), alternative schools can provide critical support and build a Caring School Community through their ability to provide small class sizes, positive climate, shared vision, and student participation in the governance structure. An Accelerated high school is an alternative school in which

- The staff is committed to educating at-risk students by sharing control of the learning process with the students and parents.
- The atmosphere is warm and accepting for staff, parents, and students.
- All members feel a sense of belonging and a sense of value.
- Students and staff create bonds of caring and looking after each other through taking the time to really get to know one another.
- All curriculum is focused and challenging.
- The academic expectations are high for *all* students.
- All students are treated as unique and worthwhile individuals.
- Generosity, respect, and responsibility are practiced by staff, students, and parents.
- Students, staff, and parents view their school as a family.
- Wraparound services for students and their families are provided to help students stay in school.

Studies indicate alternative schools with a Caring Community focus have realized the following positive results:

- Student attendance rates improve.
- Violent and aggressive student outbursts decrease.
- Students perceive themselves to be more academically capable than they were in the traditional high school.
- Self-esteem rises and discipline problems decrease.
- Students' emotional, intellectual, social, and physical needs are met and students become bonded to the school.
- Students' achievement is greater than when they were enrolled at the traditional school.
- Drug and alcohol use decrease. (Barr & Parrett, 1997)

The Accelerated Schools Philosophy

The Accelerated Schools philosophy and process give at-risk students some control over their learning process and environment. It teaches them to work collaboratively, solve problems, and take personal responsibility for their decisions. Students respond enthusiastically to participatory experiences, designing their projects to show mastery of academic material and information, and using *multiple intelligences* to find solutions to the problems posed. This philosophy is based on three principles:

- Unity of purpose
- Empowerment with responsibility
- Building on strengths

The Accelerated high school has its foundation in the Accelerated Schools philosophy developed by Dr. Henry Levin and his associates at the Stanford University National Center for the Accelerated Schools Project. The Accelerated Schools philosophy and process are detailed in Dr. Levin's book, *The Accelerated Schools Resource Guide* (Hopfenberg et al., 1993).

The Accelerated Schools model is designed to transform existing schools into Accelerated schools. This model has transformed many elementary and middle schools into collaborative, problem-solving settings in which students are engaged in *powerful learning experiences* using the *inquiry process*. We (the authors) have adapted the Accelerated Schools philosophy and process to create an alternative school from the ground up.

Establishing an Accelerated high school from scratch requires some modification of the normal Accelerated Schools process. All the same, we urge educators contemplating establishing an Accelerated high school to contact the National Center for the Accelerated Schools Project at Stanford University (415-723-0840) or the Missouri Accelerated Schools Center at the State Department for Elementary and Secondary Education (573-526-4037) for guidance on the project. It is vitally important for the success of the Accelerated high school that the Accelerated Schools process be conducted properly.

The Three Principles of the Accelerated Schools Philosophy

Unity of purpose is the first principle, whereby parents, students, staff, and the local community work together to achieve the vision and goals of the school. These groups of stakeholders work together in planning, designing, implementing, and evaluating the educational programs of the school. Unity of purpose emerges and changes as the needs of the school and community change over time (Hopfenberg et al., 1993). Throughout an Accelerated school, the unity of purpose can be found in staff meetings, student cooperative learning groups, powerful learning experiences that relate lessons to real-life situations, and cadre work groups.

Empowerment with responsibility shifts the responsibility for making all decisions regarding the learning process from central office staff and administration to students, teachers, and parents at the school site working together. The teachers are facilitators, challenging and guiding their cadres to explore, discuss, and reach consensus on strategies to implement solutions to problems, both academic and social, of the school. This principle teaches students, staff, and parents to be open to new ideas and to be flexible enough to change strategies or possible solutions when needed. It also helps the school family members understand what it means to be accountable for the outcomes of the decisions they make with regard to planning, designing, implementing, and evaluating projects (Eidson & Hillhouse, 1997).

Building on strengths is the third principle of the Accelerated Schools philosophy. This principle helps the students, staff, and parents identify their personal strengths and talents as well as those of other members of the group. They reflect on their strengths and decide how they can use their strengths to help the group achieve a unity of purpose and the school's vision.

The Accelerated Schools Process

Creating a Caring School Community does not happen overnight. It is a process in which the following steps must be taken:

- Taking stock of the school's strengths and weaknesses
- Creating a living vision for the school
- Forging the governance structure of the school
- Setting priorities to achieve the vision

To journey through the process, *cadres* (committees) are created for different aspects of the school and its programs. The cadres develop *action plans* using the *inquiry process*, with regard to the specific goals of each cadre to achieve the vision of the school.

The inquiry process encourages all groups concerned with achieving the school vision to think critically and solve the problems or challenges presented to them during the Accelerated Schools process. The inquiry process forces the stakeholders (students, parents, staff, and community members) to find the causes to problems and effective solutions. This process also includes evaluating the success of the action plans developed by the cadres.

According to Hopfenberg et al. (1993), the inquiry process utilizes the following steps:

- Focus on the problem at hand. Determine the causes.
- Brainstorm possible solutions to help reach the cadre goal and solve the presenting problem.
- Prioritize the possible solutions and develop an action plan using one solution at a time.
- Implement the action plan.
- Evaluate the success of the action plan. Revise the action plan or choose another possible solution if the evaluation results necessitate the revision.

The inquiry process is slow and in-depth. Every member of the cadre needs to feel accepted and comfortable enough to contribute his or her ideas and experiences. The presenting problem must be examined from every angle as to the cause and effect.

The inquiry process is used not only for solving major challenges and problems in achieving the school's vision; in the Accelerated high school, the inquiry process is also used daily in all academic and social situations by the students and staff. Using the inquiry process needs to become a way of life for students, parents, and staff to achieve their goals and bind them together as a true Caring School Community. The inquiry process is explored further in Chapter 7 on instructional techniques.

Empowering the Stakeholders

In building a Caring School Community through the utilization of the Accelerated Schools process, the stakeholders must be given empowerment with responsibility. Through empowerment with responsibility, the stakeholders become the "real owners" of their dream school. Pride, ownership, commitment, respect, cooperation, consensus, and responsibility emerge as the stakeholders work together with a unity of purpose to achieve the vision of the Accelerated high school. During the Accelerated Schools process, through the use of the three principles of unity of purpose, empowerment with responsibility, and building on strengths, the school environment evolves into a caring, nurturing, accepting community. Empowering the Accelerated high school's stakeholders to create their dream school within a Caring Community embodies the following recommendations from the NASSP and Carnegie Foundation (1996) report *Breaking Ranks: Changing an American Institution:*

- The high school will engage students' families as partners in the students' education.
- High schools, in conjunction with agencies in the community, will help coordinate the delivery of health and social services for youth.
- High schools will form partnerships with agencies for youth that support and supplement the regular programs of the school.
- A high school will regard itself as a community in which members of the staff collaborate to develop and implement the school's learning goals. (pp. 90-93)

In the first part of this chapter, we focused on creating a Caring Community through school-community partnerships with businesses, churches, social agencies and organizations, and individual community members. The remainder of Chapter 2 focuses on the leadership roles and empowerment of the principal, teachers, parents, students, and other school staff members to create a Caring School Community. The roles and responsibilities of these stakeholders are more expanded and very participatory within the Accelerated high school versus the traditional high school. Leadership is expected and cultivated in all stakeholders involved in the school.

Reshaping the Role of the Principal

Becoming a principal in an Accelerated high school demands shedding the traditional principal role, mind-set, leadership style, and absolute authority and power. The transformation from a traditional school principal to an Accelerated School principal can be a most exhilarating and liberating experience. The principalship can be a very isolating and stressful position in the traditional school in which the principal is the one who typically initiates and implements change, coordinates programs for students and staff, and still tries to find time to be the curriculum and instructional leader. For an Accelerated high school principal, the role is one of a coach, cheerleader, and collaborative team member with the other stakeholders.

The principal is still charged with ensuring that the school follows district, state, and federal policies and laws, but the principal shares the day-to-day decision making and acts on the recommendations of the school's cadres and steering committee. It is a new role of being a "consensus builder" and "keeper of the dream." This new role allows the principal freedom to really focus on curriculum and instruction and the needs of at-risk students. According to Ronald R. Edmonds (1982), the most important characteristic of an effective school is the principal's leadership and attention to the quality of instruction.

The principal of the Accelerated high school must have a high level of organizational and people skills to inspire and coach the staff in working toward a unity of purpose through consensus. He or she must believe in the inquiry process for solving problems or addressing challenging issues and areas to foster consensus building among the staff. According to Hopfenberg et al. (1993), the principal is a major dream keeper, who works with the staff to overcome burnout, frustration, and disappointments.

The Accelerated high school principal models empowerment with responsibility through his or her delegation of traditional principal duties such as discipline and determining the budget and class schedule. The principal identifies individual staff talents and utilizes them to build on the strengths of other staff members to work toward achieving the school's vision. The role of the principal in the Accelerated high school embodies the following recommendations from the NASSP and Carnegie Foundation (1996) report *Breaking Ranks: Changing an American Institution:*

- The principal will provide leadership in the high school community by building and maintaining a vision, direction, and focus for student learning.
- The principal will foster an atmosphere that encourages teachers to take risks to meet the needs of students.
- The leadership of students, parents, and others in the school community will enhance the work of the principal, who should recognize this potential for leadership by nurturing and supporting it. (p. 9)

The Accelerated high school principal coaches his or her staff members to create powerful learning experiences for students and to have a bigger personal vision for their instructional techniques. The principal sets the tone of the building as a nurturing, accepting "family" through encouraging and fostering risk taking and independence in the staff. The principal lets the staff know it is "okay" to make a mistake when it is done in trying something new to benefit the at-risk students at the school. The Accelerated high school principal empowers his or her staff to change and give feedback regularly. Most important, the principal gives his or her staff the power to share in decision making and in implementing the decisions made. He or she also shares with the staff the responsibility for the results of the decisions the team made together.

It is vitally important that the principal of an Accelerated high school be committed to the Accelerated Schools philosophy. He or she should work closely with the National Center for the Accelerated Schools Project at Stanford University or with the Missouri Accelerated Schools Project at the Missouri Department of Elementary and Secondary Education to ensure that the stakeholders are following the process correctly as they create their Accelerated high school. It is also vitally important that the principal be committed to the Caring Communities philosophy and at-risk students. He or she must have high but realistic expectations for the at-risk students in his or her charge. The principal must be willing to work with the parents of his or her students, realizing the parents can be as much at risk as the students. He or she must be attainable, available, and visible to the staff, students, and parents daily to have his or her hand on the pulse of the school.

The Accelerated high school principal must know the values, beliefs, attitudes, and needs of the community. The principal has to build strong, positive, community relations with the stakeholders of the school and the community at large. According to David Dwyer (1984), the principal must be able to "take the message of the school to the community" (p. 34). He or she must be aware of the problems, constraints, successes, strengths, and weaknesses of the community. An Accelerated high school principal should strive to help the stakeholders make the school an integral part of the community.

Empowering the Staff

Having a staff that believes in and is committed to the Accelerated Schools philosophy and the Caring Communities philosophy is a must. Every member on the Accelerated high school staff must *want* to work with at-risk teenagers and *want* to work in an alternative school. Without the "believe in," the "committed to," and the "want to" of each staff member, the effectiveness and success of the school becomes "at risk" for failure. It is not an easy task to spend 7 or 8 hours each day for 9 months of the year with teenagers who have sarcastic attitudes, drug or alcohol problems, abuse issues, hot tempers, depression, apathy, low motivation, authority problems, and high intelligence. Some days, these young people could try the patience of a saint and laugh about it! So, it is imperative that staff members of the Accelerated high school come into their job with eyes open, a heart for at-risk students, and a determination to keep reaching out to these teenagers each day.

Because most alternative schools are started from scratch, the opportunity presents itself to the principal and the rest of the hiring team to interview and hire staff members who truly want to be participatory members of the Accelerated high school family. It takes a special type of person to be effective in working with at-risk students. The following are some characteristics of effective teachers and staff for at-risk students:

- Flexible
- Highly organized
- Sensitive to the students' family lives and emotional baggage
- Cannot be manipulated
- Refrains from getting into power struggles with students
- Good sense of humor
- Enjoys being a member of a team
- Open to trying new instructional and discipline techniques
- Not afraid of failure
- Warm, nurturing, and accepting
- Knowledgeable in subject area
- Willing to create powerful learning experiences for the students
- Not afraid to put the teacher manuals on a shelf to collect dust
- Likes at-risk teenagers

Staff members in the Accelerated high school are empowered to work cooperatively with one another and build on each other's strengths as they work with a unity of purpose to achieve the school's vision. Custodians, cooks, secretaries, teachers, paraprofessionals, the principal, counselors, and any other staff members are a united team, committed to providing a Caring Community and accelerated curriculum for their at-risk students.

Empowerment with responsibility does not happen overnight with the staff in the Accelerated high school. Shared decision making, consensus building, and finding solutions through the inquiry process needs to be taught to the staff from day one. The principal and four teachers will be required to attend the training for Accelerated schools either through their state Accelerated Schools Satellite Center or the National Center for the Accelerated Schools Project.

Some staff members may be timid or uncomfortable in providing input to the group because their input has not generally been solicited in the traditional high school's top-down decision-making process. Other staff members jump right in, testing the "empowerment" part but shying away from the "responsibility" part for implementing solutions and accepting consequences for their decisions if things do not work out as planned. The principal is the key player for helping the staff become empowered with responsibility. The principal must not give in and make decisions when the staff is reluctant. The principal must also allow the staff to experience some setbacks while staff members learn to assume responsibility for the decision making at the school.

Many state departments of education are quite flexible with the rules and regulations when it comes to alternative schools. For example, we wanted to create a "family atmosphere" at the Community School. We felt strongly that elementary-certified teachers are trained in creating a nurturing "nest" for their class of students, whereas secondary-certified teachers are trained more in line with college professors, with little training in providing the family atmosphere. We received permission from the Missouri Department of Elementary and Secondary Education to utilize a combination of elementary-certified teachers and secondary-certified teachers. The results of this marriage have yielded the following positive, observable results:

- The elementary-certified teachers taught the secondary-certified teachers how to create a nurturing "nest" in their classrooms for our at-risk students. The secondary teachers' classrooms now display colorful bulletin boards; student work on the walls; plants; artwork; area rugs; learning centers; and a warm, accepting atmosphere.
- The elementary teachers have learned a tremendous amount of information about working effectively with at-risk teenagers and secondary subject matter.
- It was easy for the elementary teachers to work in the "independent study labs," in which a group of students may be working on different subjects at the same time. Elementary teachers are trained in all subject areas, whereas secondary teachers' training is more subject-specific.
- The secondary teachers coached their elementary colleagues on the secondary curriculum and state objectives for all the Accelerated high school's course offerings.
- The marriage of elementary-certified teachers and secondary-certified teachers is a marvelous blend of talent, creativity, knowledge, and community building through the inquiry process in all decision making and problem solving from two different educational training backgrounds.

We recommend readers work closely with their specific state department of education and the National or state Accelerated Schools Centers in order to be able to try innovative staffing combinations to fit at-risk students' specific needs. The alternative school movement is relatively new, but it is gaining a wide circle of respect across our nation as more and more data are collected showing positive results in keeping at-risk students from dropping out. State departments of education are more open than ever before to piloting innovative staffing combinations, assessment techniques, and criteria for awarding high school credit within the alternative school setting.

Once staff members become comfortable with shared decision making and consensus building, they truly become empowered and a transformation occurs. Collaboration, creativity, and support blossom when the staff feels empowered and is allowed to act on its decisions. The following story illustrates the initiative of an empowered staff:

> "C.B., can we see you for a minute?" a grinning Miss Sandy and Miss Emmi asked me as they walked into my office. Both of my English teachers immediately sat in the rocking chairs facing my desk, grinning from ear to ear.
> "What are you two up to this time?" I laughed, shaking my head because a visit by two or more staff members always means new ideas, approaches, or projects to try out at the Community School.
> "We're on a fact-finding mission for an idea we have," Emmi started in. "We'd like to discuss the possibility of starting a tradition for the senior class with our staff at the meeting today. We'd like to have a "senior-staff dinner" at the end of the year. We want to take the seniors to a semi-fancy, sit-down restaurant, because most of our students never have the opportunity to get dressed up and go out to dinner."
> "We need to know if we can use student activity funds for this event." Sandy added, "If the staff likes the idea, we'll discuss it with the senior class tomorrow."
> "I think we'd have enough money to cover this tradition each year through fund-raisers in the student activity account," I told them. " We only have 18 to 25 seniors each year, so I think your idea is very feasible. Looks like you two might have started a new tradition for our school!"

Traditions, innovative instructional techniques, powerful learning experiences, and a dream school can be created when the staff is empowered with responsibility. Another positive result of empowering the staff is lower staff absenteeism, burnout, and frustration. Ownership and pride emerge as the staff shares in the decision-making responsibilities of the day-to-day operations of the school, the curriculum, and the school climate.

Empowering At-Risk Students

At-risk students need to feel they have some control over their lives, their environment, and their learning process or they "turn off" to adults, the school, and their community. Temper tantrums, bad attitudes, low motivation, apathy, alienation, sarcasm, and mistrust can be decreased in at-risk students when they are given empowerment with responsibility to work toward a unity of purpose in creating their dream school. Empowerment with responsibility has to be slowly nurtured and developed in at-risk students, because most do not know how to accept personal responsibility for their actions; nor do they want to accept responsibility. But, oh, how they want the "empowerment"!

At-risk students can be empowered with responsibility through utilizing the inquiry process to solve problems or meet challenges. As the at-risk students learn and actively participate in the Accelerated Schools process with the staff and other stakeholders, they slowly begin to understand what empowerment with responsibility means and entails. They can serve on cadres or give input in their "family groups" with regard to specific issues, projects, policies, procedures, or events. Students can practice empowerment with responsibility in their classrooms by being allowed to choose topics for study or projects to conduct to show mastery of a skill or information, participating in peer tutoring, or being a classroom aide, among other things.

Cultivating Parent Involvement

It is essential that the Accelerated high school staff nurture and cultivate parent involvement and active participation in the Accelerated Schools process. Parents have an important role in helping to create this dream school. They need to be invited and encouraged to become actively involved in the formation of this new alternative school for their children. This is not an easy task for the staff and other stakeholders. Many parents of at-risk students are in at-risk situations themselves. Many of these parents have never been actively involved in their children's schools. Our conversations with parents of at-risk students reveal that many of these parents feel the same mistrust, alienation, apathy, unworthiness, and low self-esteem as their children do with regard to the traditional school system.

It is up to the staff to make the parents feel valued, important, and necessary to the success of the school and their child's education (Hopfenberg et al., 1993). The following suggestions on how to cultivate parent involvement in the Accelerated high school are a combination of ideas from the staff at the Community School, Hopfenberg et al. (1993), and Warner and Curry (1997):

- Invite parents to Accelerated Schools training sessions
- Have teachers and other staff members make personal phone calls or home visits to families to solicit their input on school issues
- Personally ask parents to work on cadres
- Initiate "Breakfast with the Staff" once a month for parents to have coffee and donuts before work to chat about their ideas, suggestions, or concerns
- Schedule parent meetings at flexible times for parents' different work schedules
- Implement special parent and family events at the school
- If space is available, set up a "Parent Room" at the school, in which parents can come to use a computer or check out reading material or videos that address issues concerning teenagers and parenting skills
- Ask parents to share their hobby or information about their career or a trip with the students
- Initiate an open-door policy to encourage parents to come visit the school as often as they like
- Implement topic meetings, parent support groups, or classes for parents at night at the school

Through active involvement, the parents begin to develop pride, ownership, and responsibility for their dream school. As they begin to feel safe, wanted, and valued at the school, at-risk parents slowly start coming to night meetings, serving on cadres, and calling the principal with their ideas and input. After 4 years, we now have many parents who call the school to ask if we can use different items they might have or to tell us about someone who would be a good speaker for the students to hear. Parents seem to "drop in" more often just to chat and visit with the office staff or principal during the day. The reason for this gradual about-face for these parents is they now trust the staff and know we care about them and their children.

Chapter Summary

The Accelerated high school is a Caring School Community that branches out to create a Caring Community with the community at large. Utilizing the Accelerated Schools philosophy and the Caring Communities philosophy together encompasses and fulfills the recommendations from *Breaking Ranks: Changing an American Institution,* a (1996) report by NASSP and the Carnegie Foundation. Within the framework of Accelerated Schools philosophy, Caring Communities philosophy, and the *Breaking Ranks* recommendations, schools can become caring and nurturing while giving each student a sense of belonging and acceptance. It is in this type of "family environment" that at-risk students excel, becoming interested and motivated to learn.

Wraparound services for at-risk students and their families enable these teenagers to stay in school and graduate. Bonds between staff, students, parents, and community members are forged and strengthened as the family becomes more trusting and stable as a result of the wraparound services and caring school environment. The school becomes viewed as a "safe home" where parents do not feel threatened, inferior, unwelcome, or useless. The Accelerated high school seeks and welcomes parents' input and involvement in all aspects of the school and its programs.

Feelings of alienation and apathy by the students are erased in a Caring School Community as the students and staff get to know each other as individuals who have worthwhile feelings and ideas. Students are encouraged to become involved in the governance and instructional programs along with other aspects of their school. As the at-risk students are empowered with responsibility and work with the staff with a unity of purpose to achieve the school's vision, trust and relationships are formed and strengthened. Students begin to realize and know in their hearts that the staff really cares about each of them.

When students realize their school is a Caring Community, discipline problems decrease, attendance rates improve, achievement improves, self-esteem rises, and motivation for learning increases. The Accelerated Schools philosophy and process produce an environment that teaches and encourages students to soar like eagles. The succeeding chapters discuss each of the steps necessary for readers to develop and implement an Accelerated high school.

3

Taking Stock
Community and School Strengths and Weaknesses

"To know where we are going, we
have to first know where we are."

C. B. Eidson
(Presenter, Mo.S.T.A.R. Conference, 1995)

Most alternative schools are started from scratch in a separate facility or set apart as a school-within-a-school located in the traditional high school building. If the school is to be housed in a separate facility, the school district will need to supply startup equipment—furniture, supplies, and materials. Both types of alternative schools can easily and effectively become Accelerated high schools through the identification and involvement of all groups of people who will be affected by the Accelerated high school. All become *stakeholders*. The following groups involved with the Accelerated high school make up the stakeholders in the Accelerated high school:

- All staff, both certified and noncertified
- All students enrolled in the school
- All parents of Accelerated high school students
- Central office personnel
- Directors of special education, Title I, staff development, and technology
- As many community members as possible
- Local board of education members
- An outside coach from an area college or university or district central office trained and mentored by the National Accelerated Schools Project

An Accelerated high school has its beginnings with the dreams of its students, parents, staff, and community members with regard to the kind of school they want *their* children and *all* children to attend. Chapter 4 explores brainstorming a dream school as the first step in creating the vision of the school. Before the stakeholders can realize their dream school or even begin planning it, they must know where the school *is* so they can begin creating the vision and achieving it.

In other words, each group of stakeholders in the school must help determine the strengths and weaknesses of every aspect of the school and community. This step of the Accelerated Schools process is called *taking stock* (Hopfenberg et al., 1993). It is during this stage that baseline data are collected and analyzed. Baseline data include more than facts gathered about various aspects of the school. They also include stakeholders' values, beliefs, attitudes, and needs with regard to the school *and* community.

It is important to remember that the Accelerated high school is not an entity in itself. This school is part of the community at large and therefore must reflect the values, beliefs, attitudes, and needs of the community. The Accelerated high school shares the vision and goals of the community. To develop a shared vision, the stakeholders must also take stock of the community's strengths and weaknesses.

Incorporating the Three Principles
of the Accelerated Schools Philosophy

Taking stock involves each of the three principles of the Accelerated Schools philosophy. Taking stock initiates the process of engaging the stakeholders in working toward a unity of purpose. The unity of purpose stage examines each dimension of the school and community to determine baseline strengths and weaknesses in order to move toward a unified vision.

The school as a whole (meaning all stakeholders) and each taking stock cadre are empowered with responsibility to use the inquiry process in their taking stock investigations. All stakeholders are given the freedom, power, and responsibility to ask questions, brainstorm, examine, and discover all pertinent information, practices, procedures, values, beliefs, and attitudes in all aspects of the areas being investigated in the taking stock process. They are given the responsibility to do a complete and thorough investigation and inquiry to answer the major question of "Where are we right now?"

Taking stock involves utilizing and building on the strengths of each student, staff member, parent, and community member participating in this process. Stakeholders have different jobs and responsibilities, based on their talents, abilities, and strengths, in investigating and gathering specific data for the various challenge areas. Utilizing the diverse talents and strengths of the group makes the process of taking stock easier and more efficient.

The Stakeholders' Journey Begins

Since taking stock is an in-depth, personal study and inquiry into the strengths and weaknesses of the school and community, it is imperative that *all* stakeholders are invited to participate in this stage. The school should hold a whole-school meeting to explain the Accelerated Schools philosophy, principles, and process and their role in creating a dream school. We have found if we call this meeting a "kickoff celebration" and combine it with a barbecue or chili dinner, the turnout has been quite good. Many stakeholders will come out of curiosity, concern, excitement, and other reasons that have to do with starting a new type of school for at-risk students. It may take some personal phone calls from the staff to invite the parents of the at-risk students who will be attending the school. Remember, these parents usually have a mistrust of schools as a result of their own personal experiences as a child as well as those of their own child. Parents of at-risk students are not accustomed to school personnel *really wanting* their presence or input into the workings and vision of the school.

At the kickoff celebration, the process of taking stock really begins in earnest. The stakeholders brainstorm in the large group as many facets, aspects, and areas of the school and community as they want to gather information about and analyze for their baseline data. After brainstorming and charting, give all participants some time to walk from chart to chart to reflect on the areas to be studied. Usually, the list of areas will be long and contain similarities and related aspects.

From our own taking stock journey and those of other Accelerated schools come the following examples of some school and community challenge clusters commonly tackled by the stakeholders:

- Curriculum
- Parent and family involvement
- Instructional delivery systems
- Facilities and grounds
- Traditional discipline procedures
- Attendance rates of the students to be involved in this new school and attendance policies, procedures, and incentives
- Funding sources and budget
- Equipment and furniture
- Supplies and materials, including reference materials and textbooks
- Available technology
- School climate
- Community wraparound services available to students, parents, and families
- Extracurricular activities
- Instructional assessment methods
- Student achievement and graduation rates
- Community demographics and socioeconomic makeup
- School governance and organization

The group then combines related areas and votes on 8 to 10 final challenge clusters to be investigated by the taking stock cadres to be formed.

Forming the Taking Stock Cadres

Parents, students, staff, and community members volunteer to serve on the various *taking stock cadres*, making sure each cadre has representation from each stakeholder group. A representative from each taking stock cadre serves on the Accelerated Schools Steering Cadre, which coordinates the entire Accelerated Schools process. The following are examples of final taking stock cadres:

- Curriculum and Instructional Delivery Systems
- Buildings and Grounds
- Community Wraparound Services
- Parent and Family Involvement
- Funding and Budgets
- Attendance
- School Climate
- School Organization and Procedures

Data Collection Activities

Individual taking stock cadres use the inquiry process to generate a list of questions to gather data on their specific subject area's strengths and weaknesses. They are seeking to understand "Where they are now." Taking stock cadres *do not* ask questions about solutions. Rather, the questions must always solicit answers for an inventory of present conditions.

For example, a taking stock cadre that is investigating attendance rates of the students to be enrolled in the Accelerated high school might develop the following questions to determine baseline data:

- Are students more prone to be absent on Mondays and Fridays than on Tuesdays, Wednesdays, or Thursdays?
- Does fall, winter, or spring have the lowest attendance rates?
- Do parents enable their children to stay home from school?
- What incentives do students have to come to school regularly?

The answers to cadre questions can be obtained through interviews, surveys, observations, or researching school records. In starting an Accelerated alternative high school, important baseline data can be obtained by conducting separate surveys and interviews with the community, parents of the at-risk students attending the school, the staff, and the students. The following examples of taking stock and vision surveys for the community, parent, and student stakeholder groups helps to generate baseline data for developing and implementing an Accelerated high school. The questions are developed with the intent to give the cadre members a solid understanding of community, parent, and student values, beliefs, attitudes, and needs concerning school and community. Sample data have been inserted in the examples that follow for the purpose of data analysis discussion. Copies of blank surveys can be found in the Resources section for readers to copy and use with their stakeholders. We urge readers to develop community, parent, and student surveys that will bring in data specific to their stakeholders' needs, attitudes, beliefs, and values.

The stakeholders of an Accelerated high school may find it easier to take stock and develop the vision at the same time. An Accelerated high school is typically created from the ground up, not from an existing school, which means data have to be collected from and by stakeholders who do not know each other well or have a history with this new school.

Sample Data From a Community Taking Stock and Vision Survey

Our school district has set a goal to prevent students from dropping out of high school before graduating and helping those that have dropped out return to school to earn their diploma. We need your input in determining the needs of the community with regard to programs and services for these students and their families. Please place a check mark (✓) by the answer that best describes your answer to the question. Thank you for your help and support in this matter.

The School District Administration

1. Our community is a safe and healthy place for families and children to live and work.

   (65%) Strongly Agree
   (20%) Agree
   (2%)   Neutral
   (13%) Disagree
   (0%)   Strongly Disagree

2. Our community has enough rental homes and apartments for low-income families.

   (10%) Strongly Agree
   (15%) Agree
   (2%)   Neutral
   (37%) Disagree
   (36%) Strongly Disagree

3. Landlords and homeowners need to clean up and fix up their property to help maintain property values and look pleasing to the community.

   (76%) Strongly Agree
   (21%) Agree
   (0%)   Neutral
   (3%)   Disagree
   (0%)   Strongly Disagree

4. This community cares about families and children in need and provides enough help to them with clothing, food, shelter, etc.

   (12%) Strongly Agree
   (34%) Agree
   (2%)   Neutral
   (32%) Disagree
   (20%) Strongly Disagree

5. Our community has many recreational facilities and activities for children and families.

   (0%)   Strongly Agree
   (6%)   Agree
   (4%)   Neutral
   (11%) Disagree
   (79%) Strongly Disagree

6. Our community has a variety of leisure-time activities for children ages 13-18.

   (0%)   Strongly Agree
   (3%)   Agree
   (4%)   Neutral
   (11%) Disagree
   (82%) Strongly Disagree

7. Our community needs a recreation center or other places for teenagers to have safe, alcohol-free activities with their friends.

   (82%) Strongly Agree
   (11%) Agree
   (4%)   Neutral
   (3%)   Disagree
   (0%)   Strongly Disagree

8. In today's society, a community that prospers economically and socially has a majority population with a high school diploma or more education.

    (29%) Strongly Agree

    (53%) Agree

    (2%) Neutral

    (11%) Disagree

    (5%) Strongly Disagree

9. A poorly educated community will not attract high-skill industry, small businesses, or new families to relocate there.

    (29%) Strongly Agree

    (53%) Agree

    (2%) Neutral

    (11%) Disagree

    (5%) Strongly Disagree

10. Teenagers who drop out of school become a financial burden to their community.

    (36%) Strongly Agree

    (49%) Agree

    (5%) Neutral

    (7%) Disagree

    (3%) Strongly Disagree

11. Education should be a priority for children and adults in order for them to become productive and responsible citizens in the community.

    (52%) Strongly Agree

    (40%) Agree

    (3%) Neutral

    (3%) Disagree

    (2%) Strongly Disagree

12. Teenagers who drop out of school tend to get into trouble in the community.

    (32%) Strongly Agree

    (43%) Agree

    (5%) Neutral

    (12%) Disagree

    (8%) Strongly Disagree

13. It is easy for teenagers in our community to buy alcohol.

    (36%) Strongly Agree

    (49%) Agree

    (5%) Neutral

    (7%) Disagree

    (3%) Strongly Disagree

14. Gangs are becoming a problem in our community.

    (5%) Strongly Agree

    (25%) Agree

    (10%) Neutral

    (45%) Disagree

    (15%) Strongly Disagree

15. Teenagers who drop out of school do not have the proper educational skills to obtain high-skill and high-paying jobs, thus costing employers more money to train these workers.

    (35%) Strongly Agree
    (46%) Agree
    (3%) Neutral
    (14%) Disagree
    (2%) Strongly Disagree

16. The school district in a community needs to find creative ways and programs to keep students motivated to remain in school and graduate.

    (76%) Strongly Agree
    (17%) Agree
    (2%) Neutral
    (5%) Disagree
    (0%) Strongly Disagree

17. Parents need to take an active role and be involved in their child's education and school as a good role model for their child.

    (76%) Strongly Agree
    (21%) Agree
    (3%) Neutral
    (0%) Disagree
    (0%) Strongly Disagree

18. Parents should be held responsible and accountable for making their child attend school each day.

    (14%) Strongly Agree
    (43%) Agree
    (15%) Neutral
    (25%) Disagree
    (3%) Strongly Disagree

19. Community members, the school district, businesses, churches, and social organizations and agencies should collaborate with each other to provide for children and families in need in the community.

    (64%) Strongly Agree
    (36%) Agree
    (0%) Neutral
    (0%) Disagree
    (0%) Strongly Disagree

20. Teenagers who drop out of school are usually bored and unmotivated by traditional teaching styles and instruction.

    (38%) Strongly Agree
    (54%) Agree
    (5%) Neutral
    (3%) Disagree
    (0%) Strongly Disagree

21. Tracking children in low, average, and high classes leads to low self-esteem and frustration for children placed in the low classes.

    (20%) Strongly Agree
    (67%) Agree
    (10%) Neutral
    (3%) Disagree
    (0%) Strongly Disagree

22. Alternative educational programs and schools that include parents, students, and staff working together to make learning interesting, fun, and motivating are needed in our community.

   (22%) Strongly Agree
   (41%) Agree
   (27%) Neutral
   (10%) Disagree
   (0%) Strongly Disagree

23. Vandalism, gangs, and violence will decrease if teenagers and their parents are actively involved in the school and community programs and activities.

   (22%) Strongly Agree
   (65%) Agree
   (5%) Neutral
   (8%) Disagree
   (0%) Strongly Disagree

24. Children need to relate real-life experiences to the academic information they learn in school to prepare and motivate them for life after graduation.

   (27%) Strongly Agree
   (53%) Agree
   (12%) Neutral
   (8%) Disagree
   (0%) Strongly Disagree

25. With the pressures, problems, and breakup of the traditional family in today's society, the schools should teach Character Education Values and organize Community Service projects for the students to teach them to "give back" to their community.

   (22%) Strongly Agree
   (51%) Agree
   (15%) Neutral
   (12%) Disagree
   (0%) Strongly Disagree

26. People feel like "winners" when they receive their high school diploma.

   (78%) Strongly Agree
   (22%) Agree
   (0%) Neutral
   (0%) Disagree
   (0%) Strongly Disagree

Sample Data From a Student
Taking Stock and Vision Survey

This survey is to be given to all Middle School and High School students to find out their ideas and feelings toward school.

Please place a check mark (✓) by the answer that best describes your answer to the question. Please fill in answers to questions requiring a written response.

Thank you for your help in this matter.

The Staff

1. I feel comfortable and accepted by the other students and staff at my regular Middle School or High School.

   (12%) Strongly Agree
   (33%) Agree
   (2%) Neutral
   (43%) Disagree
   (10%) Strongly Disagree

2. I feel close to my teachers.

   (16%) Strongly Agree
   (12%) Agree
   (6%) Neutral
   (42%) Disagree
   (24%) Strongly Disagree

3. I am involved in extracurricular clubs and activities at the regular Middle School or High School.

   (32%) Yes
   (68%) No

4. I have to work after school so I cannot participate in after-school activities.

   (78%) Yes
   (22%) No

5. I can talk to my teachers about anything that is important to me.

   (32%) Yes
   (68%) No

6. I feel a close student-teacher relationship is very important.

   (26%) Strongly Agree
   (44%) Agree
   (5%) Neutral
   (23%) Disagree
   (2%) Strongly Disagree

7. I learn best by (Please check *all* the ways you learn well):

   (22%) Lecture style
   (60%) Hands-on projects
   (41%) Class discussions
   (19%) Work/study classes
   (82%) Small group projects
   (56%) Field trips
   (2%) Making things

   (62%) Individual projects
   (13%) Reading and answering questions from textbooks
   (10%) Worksheets
   (53%) Reading newspapers, novels, magazines
   (48%) Using computers, videos, laser disks, videotaping
   (72%) One-on-one teacher instruction
   (47%) Listening to directions and information needed
   (43%) Seeing displays or visual demonstrations

8. Getting a high school diploma is important to me.

   (89%) Strongly Agree
   (11%) Agree
   (0%) Neutral
   (0%) Disagree
   (0%) Strongly Disagree

9. In a Middle School or High School with over 1,000 students, I would feel lost in the crowd or alienated.

   (41%) Strongly Agree
   (36%) Agree
   (1%) Neutral
   (12%) Disagree
   (10%) Strongly Disagree

10. I would like to have some control and choices in what I learn.

    (67%) Strongly Agree
    (30%) Agree
    (3%) Neutral
    (0%) Disagree
    (0%) Strongly Disagree

11. I feel there is a lot of student freedom in my traditional Middle School or High School.

    (10%) Strongly Agree
    (21%) Agree
    (5%) Neutral
    (38%) Disagree
    (26%) Strongly Disagree

12. Name three (3) characteristics you want your teachers to have.

    1. _____

    2. _____

    3. _____

13. I am motivated to attend school each day.

    (12%) Strongly Agree
    (23%) Agree
    (10%) Neutral
    (35%) Disagree
    (20%) Strongly Disagree

14. I generally miss _____ days of school per semester.

    (12%) 1-2 days
    (43%) 3-5 days
    (25%) 6-10 days
    (20%) More than 10 days

15. I would be more motivated to attend school at a smaller, alternative school.

    (58%) Yes
    (42%) No

16. I feel homework is important and worthwhile.

    (13%) Strongly Agree
    (17%) Agree
    (6%) Neutral
    (43%) Disagree
    (21%) Strongly Disagree

17. I complete my homework

    (10%) 100% of the time
    (30%) 40%-69% of the time
    (35%) 70%-99% of the time
    (25%) Below 40% of the time

18. I would like to attend a school with a relaxed, family atmosphere.

    (74%) Strongly Agree
    (26%) Agree
    (0%) Neutral
    (0%) Disagree
    (0%) Strongly Disagree

19. I like a colorful, "homey" classroom with bulletin boards and student work displayed.

    (20%) Strongly Agree
    (77%) Agree
    (3%)   Neutral
    (0%)   Disagree
    (0%)   Strongly Disagree

20. I would like a classroom with couches, comfortable chairs, and tables instead of desks in a row.

    (22%) Strongly Agree
    (75%) Agree
    (3%)   Neutral
    (0%)   Disagree
    (0%)   Strongly Disagree

21. I like awards and awards assemblies.

    (69%) Strongly Agree
    (26%) Agree
    (3%)   Neutral
    (2%)   Disagree
    (0%)   Strongly Disagree

22. I like field trips as part of a class project.

    (69%) Strongly Agree
    (26%) Agree
    (3%)   Neutral
    (2%)   Disagree
    (0%)   Strongly Disagree

23. I would like to attend school in the morning and work for credits in the afternoon.

    (43%) Strongly Agree
    (21%) Agree
    (6%)   Neutral
    (17%) Disagree
    (13%) Strongly Disagree

24. I would like to attend school from 7:30 a.m. until 4:30 p.m. Monday through Thursday and be off school on Friday.

    (32%) Strongly Agree
    (22%) Agree
    (10%) Neutral
    (26%) Disagree
    (10%) Strongly Disagree

25. I would like to attend school on a year-around schedule in which we would attend school 9 weeks, then have 2 weeks off, for four cycles and have 6 weeks off in the summer and 2 other weeks of vacation.

    (12%) Strongly Agree
    (35%) Agree
    (5%)   Neutral
    (25%) Disagree
    (23%) Strongly Disagree

26. I would like to attend school the hours we presently attend.

    (20%) Strongly Agree
    (29%) Agree
    (3%)   Neutral
    (25%) Disagree
    (23%) Strongly Disagree

Sample Data From a Parent
Taking Stock and Vision Survey

Please help us determine appropriate and effective programs for our district school children by completing this survey. We are trying to address the problem of students dropping out of school before graduating from high school. Please place a check mark (✓) by the answer that best describes your feelings and opinions in response to the questions.

Thank you for your help and input in this matter.

The School District Administration

1. Having my child graduate from high school is a priority to me.
   - (72%) Strongly Agree
   - (28%) Agree
   - (0%) Neutral
   - (0%) Disagree
   - (0%) Strongly Disagree

2. Parents have a strong influence on their children in today's society.
   - (23%) Strongly Agree
   - (27%) Agree
   - (6%) Neutral
   - (34%) Disagree
   - (10%) Strongly Disagree

3. I expect and want my child to _____ after graduating from high school.
   - (13%) Go to work full-time
   - (25%) Attend a junior college
   - (14%) Attend a vocational technical school
   - (36%) Attend a 4-year college
   - (12%) Join the military

4. As a parent, I want to be involved with my child's education but sometimes I do not know how.
   - (62%) Strongly Agree
   - (38%) Agree
   - (0%) Neutral
   - (0%) Disagree
   - (0%) Strongly Disagree

5. I feel ill-equipped sometimes to deal with the issues and problems of teenagers today.
   - (27%) Strongly Agree
   - (36%) Agree
   - (3%) Neutral
   - (21%) Disagree
   - (13%) Strongly Disagree

6. Teenagers seem to get bored easily in schools today.
   - (38%) Strongly Agree
   - (41%) Agree
   - (5%) Neutral
   - (11%) Disagree
   - (5%) Strongly Disagree

7. Schools should teach to each child's learning style to promote motivation and interest.

   (35%) Strongly Agree
   (63%) Agree
   (2%) Neutral
   (0%) Disagree
   (0%) Strongly Disagree

8. A positive, warm, accepting school climate is important to make students feel they belong.

   (49%) Strongly Agree
   (51%) Agree
   (0%) Neutral
   (0%) Disagree
   (0%) Strongly Disagree

9. Parents should have opportunities to provide input on all aspects of the school.

   (35%) Strongly Agree
   (63%) Agree
   (2%) Neutral
   (0%) Disagree
   (0%) Strongly Disagree

10. Schools need to make parents feel welcomed and at home there.

    (45%) Strongly Agree
    (55%) Agree
    (0%) Neutral
    (0%) Disagree
    (0%) Strongly Disagree

11. Parents should be held responsible and accountable for getting their child to attend school each day.

    (21%) Strongly Agree
    (29%) Agree
    (15%) Neutral
    (25%) Disagree
    (10%) Strongly Disagree

12. A close student-teacher-parent relationship helps form strong bonds of trust and motivation for the students.

    (43%) Strongly Agree
    (42%) Agree
    (15%) Neutral
    (0%) Disagree
    (0%) Strongly Disagree

13. I would like my child to attend a small school so as to get more teacher attention and be well known by students and staff.

    (48%) Strongly Agree
    (46%) Agree
    (6%) Neutral
    (0%) Disagree
    (0%) Strongly Disagree

14. I want my child to have a variety of choices and experiences that relate the information he or she learns at school to real-life situations.

    (49%) Strongly Agree
    (51%) Agree
    (0%) Neutral

(0%)   Disagree
(0%)   Strongly Disagree

15. Community Service should be included in the Middle School and High School curriculum.

    (26%) Strongly Agree
    (31%) Agree
    (13%) Neutral
    (25%) Disagree
    (5%)   Strongly Disagree

16. My child might achieve better at a small alternative school that allows the students more choices and input into their own learning process.

    (39%) Strongly Agree
    (40%) Agree
    (16%) Neutral
    (5%)   Disagree
    (0%)   Strongly Disagree

17. Schools should be "family oriented" and have a "family-style atmosphere."

    (48%) Strongly Agree
    (39%) Agree
    (13%) Neutral
    (0%)   Disagree
    (0%)   Strongly Disagree

18. What are some of the reasons your child has not been successful at the traditional school?

    1. _____

    2. _____

    3. _____

    4. _____

19. Name three (3) things you would like to see implemented at your child's school to make it more of a family school.

    1. _____

    2. _____

    3. _____

20. I would like communication between my child's teachers and me every 2 weeks with regard to his or her academic and behavioral progress.

    (49%) Strongly Agree
    (51%) Agree
    (0%)   Neutral
    (0%)   Disagree
    (0%)   Strongly Disagree

21. I would be actively involved in school decision making if I knew my input was really wanted and needed.

    (37%) Strongly Agree
    (40%) Agree
    (11%) Neutral
    (12%) Disagree
    (0%)   Strongly Disagree

22. I would participate in night meetings more if baby-sitting was provided for my younger children.
    (62%) Yes
    (38%) No
23. I would participate in night meetings more if transportation could be arranged.
    (59%) Yes
    (41%) No
24. I would support and participate in Parent-Student-Staff Community Service Days.
    (68%) Yes
    (32%) No
25. I would support and participate in Parent-Student-Staff School Planning sessions if I was personally called to participate.
    (73%) Yes
    (27%) No

Data Analysis Activities

Taking stock cadre members tabulate and organize the information gathered through the surveys to get a clear picture of each group's perceptions. For example, results from the surveys on the preceding pages yield the following valuable information on the values, beliefs, attitudes, and needs of the community members, parents, and students with regard to school and community:

- The majority indicate the community is a safe and healthy place to live but there is a strong need for low-income rental homes and apartments. Community members feel strongly that landlords and homeowners need to clean up and fix up their property.
- The majority indicate the community does not provide enough help for families in need and does not have enough recreational activities for teenagers.
- The majority indicate teenage dropouts negatively impact the community socially, physically, and financially. They feel parents should be responsible for their children and take an active role in getting them to attend school and graduate.

Results from the Student Taking Stock and Vision Survey indicate

- The majority of students do not feel comfortable or close to their teachers in a large school.
- The majority do not stay for extracurricular activities.
- The majority indicate a close relationship with the staff; a warm, relaxed, school atmosphere; and a small student body are important.
- Twenty-five percent of the students continuously have problems turning in homework on time or at all.
- The majority want more control over their learning process and want active learning experiences.
- The majority feel the importance of and want a high school diploma.

Results from the Parent Taking Stock and Vision Survey yield the following baseline information:

- Most parents want to help their children do well in school but do not know how. Graduation from high school appears to be a priority.
- Most parents want their child to attend a postsecondary vocational technical school or college.
- The majority want schools to teach to individual learning styles and have a warm, positive, accepting school climate.
- Most parents want communication with the staff about their child's progress.
- Twenty-five percent of the parents do not feel it is their responsibility to get their child to attend school regularly.

The taking stock cadre takes the information from all the surveys and compares it to information gathered in the other activities conducted to find common perceptions and patterns. For example, Tige Bennett, assistant director of the Connections Project at William Woods College in Fulton, Missouri, conducted a middle school and high school student survey concerning students' perceptions about their family, community, school, and peers as part of our taking stock activities. We used these data along with our needs assessment data to gather baseline data on the community, school, family, and peers. The following perceptions from our students appear to be consistent with students' and educators' perceptions about these issues as depicted in the literature.

Of particular interest to the taking stock cadre were the students' answers to the question, "To whom do you go when you have problems?" In order of preference, the students answered

1. Peers   21%
2. Parents   19%
3. Older youth   15%
4. Grandparents   14%
5. Other adults   13%
6. Teachers   10%
7. Religious leaders   8%

Note that 90% of the students did not feel they could go to their teachers when they have problems. This perception was noted in all the data collected from our various taking stock activities, so these findings were listed as priority areas.

During interviews with students, asking about their perceptions and feelings concerning their community brought some of these comments:

- "New people are not accepted very well."
- "There's nothing to do."
- "If you don't wear the right clothes and have the right name, you're out."
- "They'd be left out and made fun of if they're different."

Student perceptions about the community's attitude toward alcohol and other drug use included the following:

- "Parents don't like it but don't do anything."
- "They deny it's here. It's not real to them."
- "They overlook the problem instead of fixing it."
- "Kids learn from their parents."
- "Some parents buy it for us."

Students describe the relationship they would like to have with their teachers as

- "Mutual respect and more personal."
- "More joking around with us."
- "Friends and easy to talk to."
- "They would respect our opinions."
- "Teachers would hang out to see what we're really like."
- "Teachers would really care if you learned."
- "Teachers would have authority in the classroom but try to understand how kids really live."
- "Not just teach and go home."

Through taking stock, the cadres usually uncover common strengths and weaknesses in the different activities they conduct. From these two sample activities described on the preceding pages, data analysis would indicate common values, beliefs, attitudes, and perceptions such as the following:

- All stakeholder groups feel a close student-teacher relationship is important.
- Graduation is a priority for these groups.

Through taking stock, the cadres usually find common strengths and weaknesses with other communities and schools. These findings help to reinforce their motivation, commitment, and urgency to develop their dream school within a Caring Community.

The taking stock cadres analyze the data obtained through their data collection activities. The cadres need to look for common values, beliefs, attitudes, and needs throughout the various data collection activities. The commonalities paint a picture of "where the school and community are" and the values, beliefs, attitudes, and needs the community, parents, staff, and students hold dear. The taking stock information helps the stakeholders forge the vision of the Accelerated high school to complement the vision of the community at large.

Chapter Summary

To create a living vision and set priorities to achieve the vision, the stakeholders must determine the strengths and weaknesses of the school and community. The stakeholders need to find out "where they are" before they can create their dream school and Caring Community.

The taking stock process involves researching, interviewing, surveying, observing, and analyzing data from all aspects of the school and community. During this process, not only are valuable information and new understandings discovered but bonds are also created among stakeholders serving on the cadres. Parents, students, staff, and community members learn the values, beliefs, perceptions, and attitudes of themselves and the others in their cadre. Input is sought on each stakeholder's perceptions, feelings, and experiences.

Taking stock is an eye-opener for many stakeholders. During this journey, they may find realities about the school and community they have been blind to in the past. Many of the realities found in taking stock activities support findings in other schools and communities as seen through television reports, newspaper articles, and the literature. William Glasser wrote about schools failing children back in 1969 in his book *Schools Without Failure*. His findings are as relevant almost 30 years later as those found in our taking stock data and a review of recent literature (Barr & Parrett, 1997; Farrell, 1990; Goodlad, 1984; Kozol, 1991; Madden & Slavin, 1989).

During this step of the Accelerated Schools process, the stakeholders also discover strengths of the school and community. It is through building on these strengths with a unity of purpose and empowerment with responsibility of the stakeholders that the vision is achieved. The Accelerated high school is a Caring Community because of the collaborative partnerships created while the stakeholders journey through the entire Accelerated Schools process together.

While taking stock, the stakeholders are also collaborating on creating a living vision for the school that complements and embodies the vision of the community. For more information on taking stock, read pages 60-73 in *The Accelerated Schools Resource Guide* by Wendy Hopfenberg, Dr. Henry Levin, and Associates (1993). The next chapter discusses creating a living vision, along with the philosophy, rationale, program goals, and objectives to achieve the vision.

4

Creating a Living Vision

"The Vision is our 'Dream School.' . . .
It is like a Lighthouse . . . yet strong like an oak tree."

11th-Grade Student

The Accelerated high school is a living, breathing, ever-emerging, Caring Community. Therefore its *Vision* must be also be viewed in that manner. The vision must give purpose to the existence of the school. It truly is the stakeholders' light and direction in achieving their dream school. The vision is "Where we want to be" at the end of the Accelerated Schools process journey (Hopfenberg et al., 1993).

Although the journey never really ends, the Accelerated high school develops into a living vision that must change as the needs of the stakeholders and the community change. The vision is like a lighthouse, illuminating the paths needed to be traveled to fulfill the dream of the stakeholders. The direction of the vision grows as it reflects the values, beliefs, attitudes, and needs of the students, parents, staff, and community in our ever-changing and challenging society.

Seeds of the Living Vision

School improvement efforts must be grounded in a clear, strong vision that recognizes the needs of school stakeholders. A review of the literature finds the most effective and successful schools and other organizations are those with a vision that gives clear directions and purpose for the organization's very existence (DuFour & Eaker, 1992).

In developing the vision for the Accelerated high school, the stakeholders must let go of personal agendas and work toward a sense of shared commitment while planting the seeds that will help the vision grow, mature, and bear fruit. The "seeds" of the vision need to be specific and describe what the dream school will be in order to produce effective school reform or improvement. Studies from the business world indicate that companies with powerful visions attract and produce effective leaders, who help keep the vision alive and growing (Bennis & Nanus, 1985; Naisbitt & Aburdene, 1985). Effective schools have the reputation of building commitment, dedication, and passion in their stakeholders to work with a unity of purpose to achieve their vision.

A strong vision gives the stakeholders a solid understanding of the direction, purpose, and goals of the school and a deep understanding of their role within this framework (Barth, 1990). Thomas Peters and Robert Waterman (1982) found in their studies of successful businesses that the foundation for effectiveness is a strong, clear vision. The vision has specific goals, objectives, and values to guide the employees in their day-to-day work. The vision needs to produce ownership and pride in the school stakeholders, while empowering them with the responsibility to find innovative and sound ways in which the vision can be achieved. Pride and ownership emerge as the vision is built on the real needs and values of each stakeholder group. According to Richard DuFour and Robert Eaker (1992), genuine commitment to achieve the school's vision comes from teachers, parents, students, administrators, and community members reaching consensus on what they want their dream school to look like and then agreeing to work toward those ends.

Creating the Vision

The vision is created from baseline data collected and analyzed during the taking stock process. The data activities produce the seeds of the vision. From the baseline data, the stakeholders discover "Where we are," and as they study this information, the stakeholders brainstorm "Where we want to be." This information is the basis for the creation of the school's vision and the directions to achieving it.

The taking stock data in Chapter 3 indicates that parents, students, and community members feel that students need to do the following:

- Have a strong positive relationship with the teachers and other staff members
- Apply academic information to real-life situations
- Utilize technology in the learning process
- Be involved with their community
- Be motivated and challenged by active learning experiences
- Stay in school and graduate prepared for an entry-level job or post-high school education

The data collected indicate that these things are not present at the time the taking stock activities are performed. The vision depicts what the stakeholders want to work toward to achieve their dream school. The needs of the stakeholders become their vision.

Accelerated High School Vision

An example of what a completed vision, based on the taking stock data, may look like for an Accelerated high school for at-risk students is as follows:

- Accelerated high school students will develop the skills of collaboration, decision making, and problem solving through participation in powerful learning experiences in real-life situations.

- Accelerated high school students will stay in school and graduate with entry-level skills for entering the workplace, junior college, vocational technical school, or a 4-year college or university through participation in an Accelerated curriculum.
- Accelerated high school students will develop pride, ownership, responsibility, and respect for their community through applying learned academic information in community service projects.
- Accelerated high school students will broaden their knowledge base and understanding of the world outside their community through the utilization of an instructional delivery system based on interactive technology.
- Accelerated high school students will develop positive self-esteem and strong personal ability confidence levels through successful participation in an Accelerated academic curriculum.
- Accelerated high school students will develop the necessary communication and interpersonal skills, sensitivity, and empathy to interact productively and appropriately in a culturally diverse society through multicultural academic and social experiences.
- Accelerated high school students will achieve the necessary skills and understanding to enable them to develop strong, appropriate relationships with adults through bonding, team-building experiences, and the day-to-day working experiences with the staff.

The vision cadre consists of a diverse group of stakeholders with strong leadership abilities. This group possesses the ability to examine issues, barriers, ideas, and different points of view with regard to the impact on the Accelerated alternative high school. Representatives from the following stakeholder groups should be included in the vision cadre:

- Parents
- Students
- Teachers
- Principal
- Superintendent or assistant superintendent
- The local board of education
- The community
- Outside coach

The responsibility of the vision cadre is to examine the lists of ideas describing the dream school that was generated by all the school stakeholders and cluster them into common patterns and themes. From these general clusters, the vision cadre then refines the ideas into specific statements of "Where we want to be." The vision cadre presents the draft vision at a school-as-a-whole meeting, where it is accepted or revised. Throughout this process, the principal acts as the chairperson of the cadre to make sure written statements are arrived at through consensus.

Once the final vision has been accepted by all groups of stakeholders, a vision celebration is planned and implemented for all school stakeholders. The vision celebration helps to make the vision "real" and known to all the stakeholders. One school we visited had the Mother's Club make a vision quilt to hang in the gym during the celebration. Another school's students made vision scrolls to give out to everyone who attended the celebration. It is important to publicize the school's vision statement to generate public understanding and support for the new school being established.

Branches of the Living Vision

The vision is like an oak tree. It is ever growing as it weathers each storm because of its strong branches and roots. The oak is sturdy and solid, standing proud and regal among the other trees in the forest. The oak has beautiful branches that give it shape and character. The Accelerated high school's vision has many branches that give it shape and character like the oak tree. The branches give the vision integrity, beauty, strength, and direction.

The branches of the living vision include the following:

- Rationale
- Philosophy
- Goals and objectives of the program
- Staff
- Administration
- Facilities and grounds
- Accelerated curriculum
- Instructional delivery system
- Funding sources and budget
- Equipment, supplies, and materials
- Daily procedures and schedule
- Parent and community involvement
- Student and staff involvement
- School governance and organization

All of the branches share a unity of purpose with one another to achieve the vision, making it grow and mature. The vision depends on the strengths of its branches as it empowers the stakeholders with the responsibility to make their dream school a reality. Next, we discuss the rationale and philosophy branches of the vision.

The Rationale

The *rationale* for developing an Accelerated high school for students at-risk for school failure or dropping out addresses the problem or challenge areas that negatively affect the school and community. The Accelerated high school's rationale addresses major problems of "turning on" young people to learning to keep them from dropping out of school. The rationale of a program speaks to the "real" problem in the community (Barr & Parrett, 1997).

The rationale provides a description of the problem and how it negatively affects students, parents, staff, and the community. It must be based on data collected from each stakeholder group. School and community statistics on student dropout rates, gangs, juvenile crime, out-of-school-suspensions, and out-of-home placements by the juvenile or family courts are examples of the types of statistical data that should be included. The rationale also gives examples of how the problem of teenage dropouts affects the economic, social, physical, and mental stability of the community. It speaks of future projections concerning these effects on the community if the dropout rate continues to increase each year.

After the detailed description of the problem and its impact on the stakeholders is given, the rationale offers solutions. These solutions must be supported from solid research, review of the literature, and needs assessment data. The solutions should help achieve the school and community vision. A general description of the program is offered to show how the solution will positively impact the problem of an increasing population of teenage dropouts.

For writing the narrative of the rationale, it may be helpful to use the following points as a guide:

- Introduction of the problem
- Negative impact of the problem on each stakeholder group
- Description of the physical size of the community and workforce, together with the socioeconomic status and careers of the residents
- Description of the underlying causes and effects of the problem on the school and the community
- Description of how the traditional high school does not meet the needs of students at risk for dropping out of school
- Details of the solution, supported with review of literature data
- General program description
- Description of how the proposed program will achieve the school's vision
- Description of community collaboration to achieve the vision and the solution

The Philosophy

The *philosophy* of the Accelerated high school is another important branch of the vision. It is the core values, beliefs, attitudes, and needs that drive the vision (Senge, 1990). The core values, beliefs, attitudes, and needs of all the stakeholder groups are gathered during the taking stock process. The philosophy identifies the stakeholders' values and beliefs about education and gives power to the vision. The philosophy also gives direction and protection to the vision through its strong foundation of core community values and sound educational theories. The core values embodied in the philosophy are the plumb line for all decisions to be made with regard to achieving the vision.

The philosophy of the Accelerated high school must be thoroughly understood and practiced by the stakeholders. It must run through the veins of the total school operation and be recognizable in the daily routine of the school. The philosophy requires specific behaviors and attitudes to be present to shape the character of the stakeholder dream school.

An Accelerated high school is predominantly designed and implemented to address the needs of students at risk for school failure who commonly drop out before graduating or merely squeak by, never realizing their full potential. The philosophy of such a school addresses the following values and beliefs:

- Education is a necessity and therefore graduating from high school is a priority.
- All people need to feel valued, accepted, and worthwhile.
- All people need to feel that what one does makes a difference to others, the school, and the community.
- All people need to be treated with dignity and respect.
- At-risk students need an orderly and healthy atmosphere that is conducive to learning.
- At-risk students need to learn self-discipline, self-motivation, and commitment to themselves and others.

- At-risk students need to have some control over their learning process.
- At-risk students need active learning experiences to construct knowledge and build on their strengths.
- Staff, parents, and community members need to model the importance of becoming lifelong learners for students.
- At-risk students need an Accelerated and challenging curriculum to "turn them on" to learning.
- Academic information and skills need to be applied to real-life situations to promote and foster critical thinking and problem-solving skills in students.
- At-risk students need to build close bonds with adults at school and in the community.
- At-risk students need a variety of nontraditional instructional techniques to keep them interested and motivated to learn.
- Communication between stakeholders is extremely important to keep the vision alive and growing.
- Parent and community involvement is valued and necessary to the success of the school.
- Stakeholders have high academic and behavior expectations for students and staff.
- Parent commitment and support is required and expected in order to achieve a cohesive school community.
- The school needs to be a Caring Community.
- At-risk students need to be given instruction and opportunities to show mastery through their specific cognitive learning style.

The philosophy not only describes the core values and beliefs of the stakeholders, it also describes the *educational theories and philosophies* that will be employed to achieve the vision. The educational theories and philosophies should complement the stakeholders' values and beliefs to drive the vision and build their dream school.

The Accelerated high school is built on the foundation of the Accelerated Schools philosophy and the Caring Communities philosophy. Within the framework of the alternative school, there are other educational theories and philosophies that are woven into the fabric of the school to help achieve the vision. The *Constructivist* theory and *multiple intelligences* theory work well to enhance the Accelerated Schools philosophy and the Caring Communities philosophy.

The Constructivist theory embodies all three principles of the Accelerated Schools philosophy of unity of purpose, empowerment with responsibility, and building on strengths. It is not an educational theory; rather it is a theory on how children construct knowledge and learn. It advocates that the school organization, philosophy, and climate be focused on the following:

- Being student-centered
- Fostering student exploration and curiosity in "applied learning" versus textbook memorization of facts
- Encouraging student independence and risk taking in learning to become problem solvers
- Fostering an environment in which students gain new knowledge and understandings through internalizing new information and acting on it to solve problems
- Utilizing adult role modeling to show students how to become self-starters and problem solvers

- Encouraging student interactions with adults and other students when exploring and discovering their world
- Creating active learning experiences for students
- Adapting the curriculum to fit the needs and values of the students
- Valuing students' ideas and viewpoints
- Developing and utilizing authentic assessment techniques

The Accelerated Schools philosophy embraces the Constructivist theory and view on gaining new knowledge and learning. If students are given empowerment with responsibility for the learning process and constructing new knowledge, the relevance and value of learning becomes internalized in them. Utilizing the Constructivist theory, students are able to work cooperatively, learning to collaborate and reach consensus as they work toward a unity of purpose in achieving the vision and purpose of the school.

The Constructivist theory also fosters the third Accelerated Schools principle, building on strengths of students, adding knowledge as the students explore and learn about the world around them.

The multiple intelligences theory meshes easily with the Accelerated Schools philosophy. The Accelerated high school's philosophy embraces the stakeholders' values of applying academic information to real-life situations and utilizing active, participatory instructional techniques. The stakeholders' values also include providing students with the opportunities and instructional techniques that allow students to show mastery through their specific cognitive learning style. With the inclusion of multiple intelligences theory in the school's philosophy, students are able to apply new understandings and new knowledge to solve real-life problems through utilizing the seven intelligences:

- Intrapersonal intelligence
- Interpersonal intelligence
- Kinesthetic intelligence
- Verbal/linguistic intelligence
- Musical/rhythmic intelligence
- Logical/mathematical intelligence
- Visual/spatial intelligence (Gardner, 1983)

The Accelerated high school's philosophy also finds support from the findings of Joseph S. Renzulli (1994), which indicate the following:

- The role of the learner in the learning process affects achievement and motivation.
- Students feel positive about school when they have some control over their learning process.
- Cooperation and motivation increase when students are allowed to investigate and solve real-life problems through group work.
- Academic, personal, and social growth increase when alternative classroom and school organization is employed.

Another study that complements and can be easily integrated and implemented throughout the Accelerated Schools principles is the NASSP and Carnegie Foundation (1996) report, *Breaking Ranks: Changing an American Institution*. The report's recommendations should be addressed in the school's philosophy as a vehicle to help build the stakeholders' dream school. The recommendations, based on decades of research on how people learn and utilize knowledge, center on sound, natural ways young people gain knowledge and learn, utilizing avenues such as the following to obtain new understandings:

- Learning needs to be personalized and approached through each student's specific cognitive learning style.
- Learning should engage students' curiosity and motivation.
- High schools need to have small student populations so as to provide the opportunity for students to develop close relationships with their teachers.
- Students need to learn to apply what they know to real-world problems and issues.
- The daily school schedule needs to be flexible and have larger segments of time for in-depth study.
- The curriculum and teaching strategies must utilize technology to the highest degree possible.
- Assessment for student knowledge and understanding should be authentic.
- Participation and collaboration between the school, staff, parents, students, and community is necessary in all aspects of the school organization and program.

The philosophy of the Accelerated high school should reflect the core values and beliefs of the stakeholders. The values and beliefs lay the foundation for

- School climate
- Daily procedures
- Staff-student relationships
- Governance structure
- Stakeholders' involvement, responsibilities, and relationships to the school
- Curriculum to be taught
- Extracurricular activities
- Academic expectations
- Behavior expectations
- Skills required for entry-level jobs in the community and outside the community
- Graduation requirements

The philosophy must also include the educational theories and philosophies that are effective with students at risk for school failure. The educational theories and philosophies are the vehicles that drive the following:

- Use of technology
- Daily schedule
- Authentic assessment activities
- Learning process
- Staff development activities
- Physical setup of the school and classrooms

The philosophy must be practiced daily in the school by the staff, students, parents, and community members to achieve the vision. It allows the stakeholders to know and understand their role in the school and the values and beliefs of the school and community. The philosophy enables the stakeholders to understand the educational theories and philosophies that are the foundation of the school. The philosophy drives and protects the vision of the Accelerated high school.

Chapter Summary

For any high school to be effective and successful in educating teenagers, it must have a strong vision of "Where the school wants to be." Because the Accelerated high school is an alternative school for students at risk for school failure, its vision must be extremely powerful and created jointly by students, staff, parents, and the community through consensus. The vision is developed from the baseline data collected and analyzed during the taking stock process.

The vision is represented by the values, beliefs, attitudes, and needs of the stakeholders. It describes the stakeholders' dream school for students who attend the Accelerated high school. The vision tells the stakeholders, "This is what we need to achieve through the day-to-day operations of the school." The vision is living, growing, emerging, and changing as the values, beliefs, attitudes, and needs of the stakeholders grow and change. It must be reviewed and revised when necessary to meet the needs of at-risk students in today's and tomorrow's ever-changing and demanding society.

The vision is solid and strong like an oak tree, able to weather storms. The vision has many branches that help it take shape and give it character and integrity. This chapter included discussions of two of the vision's branches, the rationale and the philosophy of the Accelerated high school.

The rationale describes the problem or challenges facing at-risk students. It describes how these problems or challenges negatively impact the school, staff, students, parents, and the community emotionally, socially, financially, and physically. Finally, the rationale offers a solution to the problem and gives a brief overview of the proposed program solution.

The philosophy describes the values, beliefs, attitudes, and needs of the stakeholders that impact and drive the vision. It also describes the educational theories and philosophies that are the foundation of the Accelerated high school. The philosophy must permeate every aspect and plan for the school to achieve the vision. The stakeholders must know, understand, and live the philosophy each day as they create their dream school.

The vision, with all its branches, is placed under a governance structure to ensure a safe, orderly, accepting, and productive school environment. The governance structure guards the vision and keeps the stakeholders and the programs on the journey to "Where we want to be." Chapter 5 discusses the various components and aspects of the Accelerated high school's governance structure.

5

Forging the Governance Structure of the School

"Hold fast to dreams
For when dreams go
Life is a barren field
Frozen with snow."

Langston Hughes (1902-1967)
(Petras & Petras, 1995, p. 73)

The *governance structure* of the Accelerated high school is the dream keeper of the school. It ensures through the utilization of the three principles of the Accelerated Schools philosophy that the vision is achieved and dream school is built. The governance structure is set up in such a way as to foster open communication and feelings of acceptance and belonging, along with truly shared decision making among the stakeholders, enabling them to work toward a unity of purpose. The governance structure empowers all the stakeholders with the responsibility for the following aspects of the school:

- Educational process
- Educational program
- Daily procedures
- Curriculum and technology
- Instructional techniques
- Discipline techniques
- School climate
- Building of bridges from home and community to the school
- Development of a Caring Community in the school and in the community at large
- Wraparound services for students and families

The governance structure meshes the stakeholders' talents and abilities. It builds on their strengths as it guides the stakeholders through the Accelerated Schools process while creating a true Caring Community and Accelerated high school for students at risk for school failure.

The majority of Accelerated schools in America are elementary and middle schools. These schools generally have been in existence many years before deciding to become a part of the National Accelerated Schools Project with Dr. Henry Levin of Stanford University. The stakeholders in these schools have a history

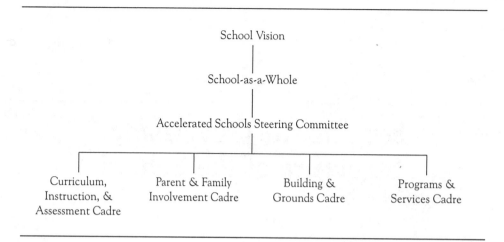

Figure 5.1. Accelerated Schools Governance Structure

together, which makes it easier to set up the governance structure and set priorities to create their dream school.

The Accelerated high school as an alternative school for at-risk students is typically started from scratch. The parents, students, and staff do not know each other at the outset. Developing and implementing their dream school can seem overwhelming to the new stakeholders the first year.

Often, the parents of at-risk students do not have a history of being involved in their child's education or school. Many of these parents have had less than memorable experiences in school as children and therefore they do not feel comfortable giving their ideas and input in cadres at first. It is for this very reason that the governance structure is so important to keep the dream alive and on the correct path to making it a reality.

Components of the Governance Structure

Because the Accelerated high school combines and meshes the Accelerated Schools philosophy and the Caring Communities philosophy, the governance structure may look a little different from that of other Accelerated schools. Generally, the Accelerated Schools governance structure concerns only a specific school and may look something like that shown in Figure 5.1 (Hopfenberg et al., 1993, p. 87).

The Accelerated high school's governance structure also includes the Caring Communities Steering Cadre and its working cadres. The school district programs such as Titles I, II, IV, and VI; special education; Homeless; and Migrant can be cadres that link into the Caring Communities Steering Cadre. For example, the Accelerated high school's governance structure may take the form shown in Figure 5.2.

The Accelerated High School/Caring Communities Steering Committee differs from the Vision Steering Committee and the Taking Stock Steering Committee. This steering committee is formed after taking stock and creating the vision. The Accelerated High School/Caring Communities Steering Committee is the permanent steering committee that oversees the continuous work of all the cadres and

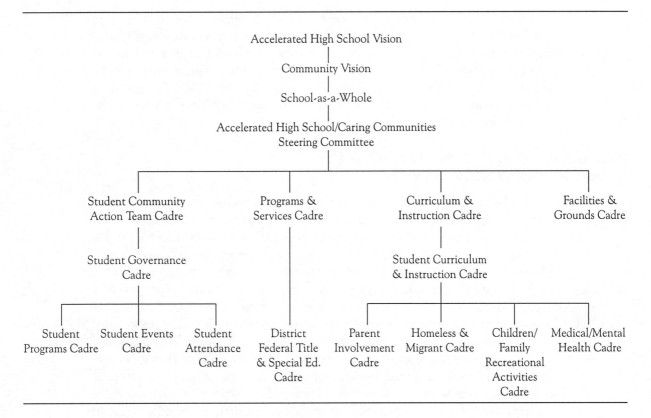

Figure 5.2. Accelerated High School Governance Structure

NOTE: Family Groups give input to each of the student cadres.

ensures that all stakeholders are working toward a unity of purpose in achieving the school's vision. Membership on this committee is voluntary and should include but is not limited to the following representatives:

- The school principal
- One central office staff member
- One or two representatives from each cadre (This may be a student, parent, staff member or a community member who is serving on the cadre.)
- One or two students not serving on any cadres
- One or two parents not serving on any cadres
- Social worker from county or state social services agency
- Juvenile officer
- Police officer
- District health coordinator
- Community businesspeople
- District director of technology
- District director of special federal programs
- Outside coach
- Community social welfare organizations and agencies
- Church pastors
- Newspaper editor
- City government official
- District staff development director
- One member of the local board of education

The steering committee meets one to two times per month to carry out its duties and responsibilities for the school-as-a-whole. This committee is the main keeper of the dream in that it oversees the total school operation, making sure all activities lead toward achieving the school's vision. The following examples of the responsibilities and duties of the Accelerated High School/Caring Communities Steering Committee are a combination of the responsibilities developed by Hopfenberg et al. (1993) and us.

Responsibilities of the Accelerated High School/ Caring Communities Steering Committee

1. The steering committee keeps the lines of communication open between each cadre and the school-as-a-whole by being the connecting link to all parts and entities within the governance structure. Cadre representatives report on cadre activities, issues, solutions, and so on to the steering committee, as do other representatives from community businesses, churches, agencies, and organizations.

2. The steering committee develops action plans utilizing the inquiry process to provide wraparound services for students and families in crisis. The Caring Communities Cadre refers specific students and families needing services in order to keep each family together and help break cycles of family dysfunction so the students can successfully stay in school through graduation. Representatives serving on the steering committee decide on needed and appropriate services, along with the goals and strategies to help each referred family become stable and independent. The following story illustrates this aspect of the responsibilities of the Accelerated High School/Caring Communities Steering Committee:

A worried 14-year-old ninth-grade boy wrote a letter to a teacher who served on the Homeless Cadre. In the letter, the ninth-grader Max wrote about the plight of his classmate Jake and Jake's family. Max was greatly concerned that Jake and his family could not pay their rent and were forced to live in a tent in a remote part of the school district. Jake had confided in Max the day before, describing the conditions and problems facing his family. Jake's dad was disabled and could no longer work in construction. Neither parent had finished high school so their job opportunities were limited. The family received food stamps and Jake's dad did odd jobs to buy gas for their truck. The family consisted of the two parents; Jake, age 14; and three younger sisters, ages 4 through 11. They had been living in the tent since late September. At the time of Max's letter, it was the middle of November. Max concluded his letter by asking the teacher to present Jake's case to the Homeless Cadre to help this family find housing before the snows came. The Homeless Cadre gathered more information on the family's situation. Representatives from the Homeless Cadre met with Jake's family and asked them if they wanted services to help them get back on their feet. The parents eagerly agreed to letting the Homeless Cadre refer their case to the steering committee for some much needed help.

The Homeless Cadre representative serving on the Accelerated High School/Caring Communities Steering Committee placed this family on the agenda for the next meeting. She then gave a report and family assessment to the steering committee. Utilizing the inquiry process, the committee reached consensus on an action plan to help Jake and his family. The steering committee was able to secure the following services for Jake's family:

- The family received 90-day temporary housing at the community's homeless shelter.

- Social Services obtained medical and dental care for the parents and children.
- Jake's mother and father were enrolled in the community college's GED program by the school district's Director of Special Services. The homeless shelter provided baby-sitting for the children while the parents attended the GED classes at night.
- A church adopted the family and provided clothing, winter coats, and shoes for the children and parents.
- Two businesses offered the parents full-time day jobs at minimum wage.
- After the 90-day temporary housing was over, the homeless shelter, along with the social worker from the Division of Family Services, helped Jake's family secure HUD housing in the community.
- Family counseling was provided by a mental health agency to help stabilize the family. Jake's mother was treated for depression and the 8-year-old daughter was treated for attention deficit disorder.
- The school provided before- and after-school care for the elementary school-age children. The 4-year-old was enrolled in the school district's Title I preschool program in the mornings and Head Start in the afternoons.

3. The cadres write proposals for action plans they want to implement to solve a problem or challenge area. They submit the proposals to the Accelerated High School/Caring Communities Steering Committee. The steering committee discusses the proposals, revises them if necessary, and presents them at the monthly school-as-a-whole meetings to be voted on by all the school stakeholders.

4. The steering committee keeps all cadres and other groups working toward a unity of purpose to achieve the school's vision. Cadres submit monthly meeting summaries to the steering committee to monitor their progress and ensure that the inquiry process is being used correctly.

5. All central office information and district, state, and federal policies and procedures are given to the steering committee to disseminate to each cadre and other groups involved with the Accelerated high school. Monthly stakeholder newsletters are written by the steering committee to keep everyone informed about the programs and activities being developed and implemented. Information is given to the community's newspapers each month to keep the community aware of the programs, activities, and decisions being made at the school. Cadre meeting minutes, update reports, and proposals are posted in the school for all stakeholders to read.

6. Accelerated High School/Caring Communities Steering Committee is responsible for providing stakeholder training in the areas of collaboration, consensus, the inquiry process, the Accelerated Schools philosophy, the Caring Communities philosophy, group dynamics, and program development. Many of the stakeholders will not have had experience working on collaborative, shared decision-making teams. Traditionally, parents, students, and staff have not been given opportunities to provide input and have not been made to feel their ideas or values are worthwhile. The erroneous assumption has been that only qualified educators can decide what is in the best interest of children and what makes a school effective and successful. The Accelerated Schools philosophy values parents, students, and staff ideas and feelings. All stakeholders are important to the effectiveness and success of the school. The steering committee's responsibility is to provide information and skill training for the stakeholders in an accepting and nurturing environment in order for each person to feel comfortable and confident enough to express his or her ideas in a group setting.

Sample Governance Structure Forms

The following forms are used by the Accelerated High School/Caring Communities Steering Committee and each cadre to plan, revise, and monitor the governance structure's progress toward achieving the school's vision. Cadre representatives serving on the steering committee bring their cadre's action plan and minutes of their meetings to the steering committee meeting each month. The steering committee checks the progress of each cadre and records it on the Steering Committee Cadre Monitoring Form. These forms are then displayed on the stakeholder bulletin board for all stakeholders to view.

The cadre action plans and Steering Committee Cadre Monitoring Forms are discussed at the school-as-a-whole meetings each month. The forms are then placed in the Accelerated Schools scrapbook or binder for the public to read. The Caring Communities Family Plan is confidential and is not discussed at the school-as-a-whole meetings or placed in the Accelerated Schools scrapbook.

ACCELERATED HIGH SCHOOL/
CARING COMMUNITIES STEERING COMMITTEE
CADRE MONITORING FORM

Cadre Name: _____ Date: _____

Goal(s):   Date: Progressing/Met:

_____   _____   _____

_____   _____   _____

_____   _____   _____

_____   _____   _____

_____   _____   _____

Strategies: Date: Progress/Completed:

_____   _____   _____

_____   _____   _____

_____   _____   _____

_____   _____   _____

_____   _____   _____

Evaluation Results:

_____

_____

_____

_____

_____

_____

_____

_____

_____

_____

_____

CADRE ACTION PLAN

Cadre Name: _____   Starting Date: _____

Revision Date: _____   Ending Date: _____

Presenting Problem:

_____

_____

Baseline Data:

_____

_____

Goal:

_____

_____

Strategies: Timeline: Provider:

_____   _____   _____

_____   _____   _____

_____   _____   _____

_____   _____   _____

Evaluation Activities:

_____

_____

Results:

_____

_____

Cadre Members' Signatures:

_____   _____   _____

_____   _____   _____

_____   _____   _____

CARING COMMUNITIES FAMILY PLAN

Family Name: _____ Date: _____

Address: _____ Phone: _____

_____ Zip Code: _____

Mother: _____ Age: _____   Father: _____ Age: _____
_____   _____

Children: _____ Ages: _____   Children: _____ Ages: _____
_____   _____

_____   _____

_____   _____

Case Manager: _____

Presenting Problem:

_____

_____

Goal:

_____

_____

Strategies: Provider: Timeline:

_____   _____   _____

_____   _____   _____

_____   _____   _____

Progress Report or Conclusion:

_____

_____

Steering Committee Members' Signatures:

_____   _____   _____

_____   _____   _____

_____   _____   _____

The Outside Coach

The *outside coach* is usually someone affiliated with a college or university that is involved with the National Accelerated Schools Project. The outside coach may also be someone in the central office in the school district but not employed at the Accelerated high school or someone from a different school district. The duties and responsibilities of the outside coach are to help the Accelerated high school keep on track during each stage of the Accelerated Schools process and monitor the progress of the governance structure. The rationale for having an outside coach is that this person will remain objective and see to it that the Accelerated Schools philosophy is followed correctly in order to achieve the vision of the school.

The Student Governance Cadre

The *Student Governance Cadre* is another component of the Accelerated high school's governance structure. This cadre is very student-centered and student-driven. The Student Governance Cadre consists of the principal, one teacher, and one student representative from each "Family Group." The Student Governance Cadre has two major responsibilities:

1. This cadre develops and implements *behavior action plans* with students who are referred to this cadre for minor-to-moderate discipline problems. (See Chapter 8 for a more detailed description of this specific responsibility of the Student Governance Cadre.)

2. The Student Governance Cadre represents the entire student body. This cadre has the same duties and responsibilities as the main Accelerated High School/Caring Communities Steering Committee with regard to the student cadres. The Student Governance Cadre sends student-generated proposals to the appropriate stakeholder cadre for consideration. The stakeholder cadres, which consist of parents students, staff, and community members, accept, reject, or revise the proposal and send it to the Accelerated High School/Caring Communities Steering Committee for consideration.

The Student Governance Cadre utilizes specific forms. One set of forms is used for student behavior referrals to develop action plans with the student. The other form is the cadre action plan form that is used in the stakeholder cadres. Sample student governance forms are shown here and in the Resources section at the end of the book for readers to copy.

STUDENT GOVERNANCE CADRE STAFF REFERRAL

Student Name: _____ Date: _____

Presenting Problem: _____

_____

_____

_____

_____

_____

_____

_____

Is this student already on Official Probation? _____

Have the parents been contacted by staff members? _____

    Contact dates: _____ _____ _____ _____

    Results: _____

    _____

Staff Signatures:

_____   _____

_____   _____

_____   _____

_____   _____

_____   _____

_____   _____

STUDENT GOVERNANCE CADRE ACTION PLAN

Student Name: _____ Date: _____

Initial Action Plan: _____ Revised Action Plan: _____

Goals:

    1. _____

    2. _____

    3. _____

Objectives:

    1. _____

    2. _____

    3. _____

    4. _____

Strategies:

    1. _____

    2. _____

    3. _____

    4. _____

    5. _____

Date of Next Meeting: _____

(Copy this page for each week's charting)

STUDENT REFLECTION LOG

Student Name: _____ Start Date: _____

Date: Reflections of daily progress toward goals:

_____   _____

_____   _____

_____   _____

_____   _____

_____   _____

_____   _____

_____

Personal rating of this week's progress:

Successes:

_____

_____

_____

_____

_____

_____

_____

Pitfalls:

_____

_____

_____

_____

_____

_____

_____

STUDENT GOVERNANCE CADRE PARENT NOTICE

Student Name: _____   Date: _____

Your child has been referred to the Student Governance Cadre for the following behavior problems, which are consistently violating the Commitment Contract he/she signed as a student in this school:

1. _____

2. _____

3. _____

4. _____

The Student Governance Cadre has recommended the following strategies to help your child decrease these behaviors and honor his/her Commitment Contract:

1. _____

2. _____

3. _____

4. _____

The Student Governance Cadre would like to meet with **you** and **your child** to review the progress your child is making toward meeting these goals.

Parent Conference Date: _____

Time: _____   Place: _____

Thank you for your commitment as a parent to your child's education and to this school. We look forward to meeting with you and your child on the above date.

Student Governance Cadre Members:

_____   _____

_____   _____

_____   _____

_____   _____

_____   _____

Other Student Cadres

The student cadres consists of one teacher, one paraprofessional, and 10 to 15 students. Each cadre utilizes the same procedures and inquiry process as the stakeholder cadres. Students are given the opportunities for leadership, in-depth research activities, problem solving, creativity, and ownership without the fear or hesitancy that can be brought on by working with parent, staff, and adults from the community. One volunteer representative from each student cadre serves on the Student Governance Cadre and one or two student representatives serve on each of the stakeholder cadres.

Student Community Action Team Cadre

The *Student Community Action Team Cadre* reports directly to the Accelerated High School/Caring Communities Steering Committee. This cadre consists of one teacher and one representative from each Family Group. Two representatives from the Student Community Action Team Cadre serve on the Accelerated High School/Caring Communities Steering Committee.

The Student Community Action Team Cadre receives ideas and input on all Community Service projects the students want to develop and implement. Proposals to this cadre are written on action plan forms by students participating in Community Service Learning classes. (All students participate in this class from 8th through 12th grade. See Chapter 7 for a description of the Community Service Learning curriculum.)

Family Groups

Family Groups are an integral part of the Accelerated high school's governance structure. A Family Group consists of one adult (teacher, secretary, or paraprofessional) and seven to nine students. Students are assigned to Family Groups by personality and mixed ages like real-life families. Students stay with the same *Family Leader* (the adult) from the date they enroll in the Accelerated high school until they graduate. As students graduate or move from the school, new students are assigned their place in the Family Group.

The Family Group is a major component of the Accelerated high school because many at-risk students come from dysfunctional home situations and lack an internalized value system and stability. Often, at-risk students do not have supportive or appropriate adult role models. The Family Group at the Accelerated high school is a nurturing, loving environment where at-risk students first encounter a sense of acceptance and belonging in the school. Values such as respect, responsibility, cooperation, trust, patience, empathy, and compassion are fostered and modeled by the Family Leader.

Students and Family Leader alike are expected to treat other students and staff with respect, compassion, tolerance, and kindness at all times. Discussions and activities are provided by the Family Leader to help the students internalize and apply these values to real-life situations. We find at the beginning of the school year, students new to a Family Group make statements such as, "This Family is stupid," or "My Family Leader is a nerd." But come spring, we find statements like the following from the same students: "Don't talk about my mom [Family Leader] like that!" or "Let's invite so and so Family to have breakfast with our Family." or "My Family is so cool!"

By spending 15 to 20 minutes per day in *Family Time*, teenagers who feel alienated and outside the circle begin to bond with and build bridges to adults and other students. They begin to feel comfortable and safe enough to "let their hair down" and confide in others. They learn that a family sticks together through the good times and the bad times, always depending on each other for love and support.

Family Time is a time when the Students and their Family Leader can discuss new ideas, procedures, rules, activities, problems, or anything else the Family Group deems necessary. Every Family Group member has the right to speak without being interrupted or "put down" in front of his or her peers. The inquiry process is used during each discussion to help the students solve problems and plan strategies or activities. Values are discussed and practiced daily to provide meaning and understanding for the students.

It is through the Family Group that at-risk students learn and practice the three principles of the Accelerated Schools philosophy. Members of each Family Group work toward a unity of purpose with regard to creating a climate of belonging and caring within their Family Group. Members are empowered with the responsibility to provide input and suggestions on how to reach the school's vision and help each other achieve personal goals. Students are shown how to build on each other's strengths to achieve the goals of the Family Group and the school.

When student cadres or stakeholder cadres need student input on specific challenge areas or problems, the Family Groups are given the task of discussing the issue and providing input. The Family representatives who serve on student cadres and the stakeholder cadres bring their Family Group's input to the cadre meetings. Family Groups can also write proposals or action plans for procedures, events, or activities and submit them to the appropriate student cadre for consideration.

The Family Leader is required to keep the lines of communication open between the home and the school. He or she must make a telephone call or send a postcard every 2 weeks to each student's parents to keep the parents informed about their child's academic and behavioral progress. Some Family Leaders set up a *weekly* time to talk by phone with a parent of a specific student who might be having difficulty in some area. Parents are encouraged to call their child's Family Leader with any concerns or ideas regarding their child's educational or behavioral progress or attitude.

Chapter Summary

As stated in this chapter, the governance structure is the keeper of the dream for the Accelerated high school. Parents, students, staff, and community members are involved in every part of the governance structure. In the Accelerated high school, decision making occurs from the bottom up, in contrast to traditional high schools with top-down decision making.

The governance structure of the Accelerated high school is set up with checks and balances to provide clear parameters and channels to achieve the school's vision. The steering committee, cadres, and Family Groups have clearly defined duties and responsibilities to enable them to work toward a unity of purpose. Empowerment with responsibility is given to all stakeholders as they are taught to build on one another's strengths to create their dream school.

Once the governance structure is in place and the stakeholders have been trained in the duties, responsibilities, inquiry process, and procedures, it is time to set priorities for achieving the vision of the school. It is the duty and responsibility of the steering committee, cadres, and school-as-a-whole to plan, develop, and implement each aspect of their dream school. We call it fashioning the skeleton, muscles, and heart of the school. Chapter 6 discusses the necessary components and steps in developing and implementing the day-to-day operations and procedures of the Accelerated high school.

6

Setting Priorities
Fashioning the Skeleton, Muscles, and Heart of the School

"Forget the former things!
Do not dwell on the past.
See, I am doing a new thing.
Now it springs up; do you not
perceive it?"

Isaiah 43:18
(New International Version)

An alternative school for at-risk students *is* "new." As it is designed to meet the needs of its stakeholders, this institution needs to be built from the ground up. When designing an alternative school, the *planning team* must "forget the former things" and "not dwell on the past" educational procedures, policies, instructional techniques, grading system, and discipline techniques that are associated with the traditional high schools, because studies show they are failing to meet the educational, social, intellectual, and emotional needs of students who are living in at-risk situations or whose cognitive learning styles are different from the instructional style of their traditional high schools (Goodlad, 1984; Kozol, 1991; Madden & Slavin, 1989; Sizer, 1992; Wood, 1992).

The planning team is assembled by the superintendent of the school district immediately after the local board of education approves the development and implementation of an alternative school for students at risk for school failure. The planning team precedes the Accelerated high school's steering committee and cadres. Its chief duties are to *set priorities* to achieve the vision by fashioning the skeleton of the Accelerated high school with sound educational theories and practices that enable the alternative school to be deliberately differentiated from the traditional high school. The team should constantly communicate with and keep everyone informed of its progress.

The planning team usually consists of the principal, the staff, other district administrators, parents, a member of the board of education, students who will be attending this new school, an outside coach, and a few community members. Once the basic skeleton of the school is formed, the planning team joins other stakeholders to serve on the Accelerated High School/Caring Communities

Steering Committee, which refines the framework and adds the muscles and heart of the alternative school. The planning team utilizes the inquiry process to develop the rationale, the philosophy, and goals of the school after doing in-depth research on the problems of decreasing the student dropout rate and creating effective schools that "turn on" teenagers to learning.

Chapter 5 discussed two of the "branches" of the living vision: the rationale and the philosophy. The planning team is charged with planning and implementing the following branches:

Branches of the Living Vision

- The rationale, philosophy, and goals for the Accelerated high school
- The types of students to be served
- Student entrance criteria and application process
- The referral process, conditions for dismissal, and appropriate forms
- The total school population, grade span, and class size
- The facilities and grounds
- The resources needed to start the school
- The grading system to be used
- The attendance policy with regard to credits
- The daily schedule

Goals of the Accelerated High School

The *goals* of the Accelerated high school should reflect the vision, rationale, and philosophy of the alternative school. The goals set priorities for the stakeholders to achieve the vision of the school. Setting priorities takes the school from "Where we are" in the taking stock stage to the vision's "Where we want to be." The goals give the stakeholders direction and focus through stating specific strategies to be utilized. The following are sample goals for an Accelerated high school:

- The students will participate in an accelerated and experiential curriculum and course of study through computer-based high school courses, powerful learning experiences, small group projects, individual projects, and cooperative learning experiences to enable each student to earn a high school diploma.
- Students will develop self-pride, community pride, and school pride through participation in Community Service Learning projects.
- Lines of communication will be opened and remain open through staff phone calls, letters, or meetings with parents every 2 weeks.
- Parents will have the opportunities to become fully involved in the Accelerated high school through participation in cadres, family events, and volunteer work.
- Students will establish close bonds with the staff through participation in Family Groups, team-building experiences, and small class sizes.
- Students will be provided the opportunities to make up lost credits and become reclassified to the status of their original classification through participation in independent study labs and correspondence courses.

The Types of Students to Be Served

To create an effective and successful Accelerated high school as an alternative school, the school must first and foremost be "homegrown." Creating a homegrown alternative school means the stakeholders need to study and research the types of students who are at risk for school failure and dropping out in their school district. A review of the literature (Firestone & Rosenblum, 1988; Hirschi, 1987; Levin, 1988; Natriello, McDill, & Pallas, 1988) indicates the following close relationships:

- High dropout rates in low-socioeconomic-level families and communities
- Higher dropout rates and personal problems in teenagers not related to social status or family background
- Higher dropout rates and school factors related to failure, retentions, and alienation

The stakeholders must find out why teenagers in *their* community are leaving high school before graduating with a high school diploma. The results of their findings determine the types of students to be served in the Accelerated high school.

For example, in studying our own school district dropouts, we found that the majority of these students were of average to gifted and talented intelligence. The findings coincide with those of studies by Osborne and Brynes (1990), Durkeen, (1981), and Brooks (1980), in which 8% to 32% of the dropouts studied had IQs above 110, which was a common point used as the classification for gifted and talented.

The questions we needed to address were, "Why are our traditional high schools failing to meet the needs of this diverse gifted and talented population?" and "Why do some gifted and talented young people excel in the traditional schools whereas others become alienated, aggressive, unmotivated, frustrated, apathetic, disruptive, or even violent in the same setting?" A review of the literature combined with studying our own school district dropouts and potential dropouts yielded the following answers to those two questions:

- The traditional high schools do not allow and plan for the instructional needs of *all* students, especially gifted students who have different cognitive learning styles, which leads to school failure, low self-esteem, frustration, behavior problems, alienation, and apathy in gifted students.
- The traditional high schools are too large and impersonal to meet the social and emotional needs of all students.
- The traditional high schools typically do not provide wraparound services to help students and their families in crisis situations. Therefore, this population of gifted and talented students has the added pressures and stressors associated with dysfunctional families to cope with while trying to academically achieve in schools that do not meet their cognitive learning style and emotional needs.
- Students who are not "model students" are typically not referred to the gifted and talented programs or courses (Arnove & Strout, 1980).
- Students who are not motivated and performing at grade level are usually automatically assigned to lower-track classes, remedial classes, or vocational classes, without the staff looking into the student's intelligence, aptitudes, potential abilities, and family situation as possible reasons for low academic performance.
- Traditional high schools appear to have special programs for disabled and low-average-IQ students but not for students in the average to gifted range of intelligence who are not motivated and performing at or above grade level.

There are other at-risk factors that should be studied closely to determine the types of students to be served in the Accelerated high school. The planning team should use the inquiry process to generate a list of factors common to the students in its school district who have dropped out or who are potential dropouts. The following list of is common to many school district dropout populations and should be considered along with factors specific to the planning team's district:

Common At-Risk Factors

- Average-to-gifted range of intelligence but little academic motivation
- Socioeconomic status of the family
- Attendance, truancy, and tardiness problems
- Drug and alcohol abuse
- Physical, sexual, and emotional abuse
- Depression and suicide attempts
- Retentions
- Loss of high school credits due to inattendance or lack of effort
- Teen pregnancy
- Academic gaps in reading and math
- Transient nature of the family
- Grade point average below 2.2
- Education a low priority in the family value system

Student Entrance Criteria

As an alternative school for students at risk for school failure and potential dropouts, the Accelerated high school must be taken seriously by the stakeholders and the community at large. Too often in today's society, alternative schools are referred to as "the schools for juvenile delinquents, bad kids, losers, or the kids nobody wants in the traditional high schools." Many alternative schools have become dumping grounds for behavior and discipline problem students who are violent, aggressive, or extremely disruptive in the traditional high schools. Students are typically sent to alternative schools as punishment or the last chance to "straighten up their behavior" before being expelled from school. These types of alternative schools are doomed to failure before they open the school doors on the first day.

Students who attend alternative schools to which "all the bad kids go" are stigmatized and labeled once again. In addition to the label of "loser" comes isolation from the general student population if the alternative school is located in a separate wing of the traditional school or in a separate facility off the high school campus. Many students placed in this type of environment feel as though they are wearing a flashing neon sign reading, "I am worthless!" When they attend an alternative school labeled "loser school," a self-fulfilling prophecy occurs in which these students act like losers and eventually drop out of school. When this happens, all the stakeholders lose the battle in our schools and communities to have educated graduates.

For an alternative school to be accepted and taken seriously by its stakeholders and the community at large, it must be credible and have a positive image in the eyes of the community. Through the utilization of the Accelerated Schools philosophy meshed with the Caring Communities philosophy, an alternative school gains credibility and validity as it becomes an Accelerated high school. Every aspect of an Accelerated high school is student-centered, focused on academic excellence and social responsibility. It must be viewed by the stakeholders as a "privilege school" to break the image of a "loser school."

The student entrance criteria must be specific in describing the types of students to be served and to be allowed entrance into the Accelerated high school. A sample of an Accelerated high school's student entrance criteria may look like the following in the student handbook and school brochure:

The Accelerated High School's Student Entrance Criteria

The following criteria *must* be met for a student to be accepted in the Accelerated High School:

1. The student must have an IQ of 100 or above.
2. The student must have a minimum fourth-grade reading comprehension level.
3. The student must show that his/her achievement is not keeping up with his/her capability based on an IQ of 100 or greater in relation to grades, credits, teacher/parent observations, and informal and standardized test scores.

A student at the Accelerated High School *must* meet at least two (2) of the following criteria, along with the three required criteria above:

1. The student has lost credits due to attendance problems, truancy, not doing homework, lack of effort, or dropping out of school.
2. The student may feel alienated at the traditional high school *due to its population size or other reasons and/or does not participate in high school activities because of feelings of not belonging.*
3. The student may come from a dysfunctional family situation and needs the support and nurturing that occurs at the Accelerated High School.
4. The student suffers from depression, agoraphobia, or other mental illness and needs a small, family-like environment in which to function academically and socially.
5. The student is recovering from drug or alcohol abuse or physical, sexual, or emotional abuse and needs a small, accepting, nurturing environment to help in his/her recovery process.
6. The student needs a different instructional delivery system that is compatible with his/her cognitive learning style to achieve up to his/her full potential and capabilities.
7. The student may need the flexible schedule of the Accelerated High School to allow the student to work to help financially support his/her family.
8. The student meets Title I eligibility and has not been academically successful in the traditional school.
9. The student has a diagnosed learning disability and/or behavior disorder and has a minimum fourth-grade reading comprehension level.
10. The student is able to function academically and socially in a less structured school environment.
11. The student has difficulty with peer and adult relationships and authority figures.
12. The student has continuous in-school suspensions and out-of-school suspensions in the traditional high school.

The Referral Process

A prospective student for the Accelerated high school may be referred from either the district middle school or high school by teachers, administrators, counselors, parents, Division of Family Services, doctors, the student himself or herself, or any other agency working with the student or family. As part of the referral process, information concerning the student's overall performance at the traditional school is compiled by the counselor at the traditional middle school or high school. This application file includes the following:

- Application form completed by the student
- Referral packet completed by all of the student's teachers
- Permanent records
- Any other information pertinent to the student's admission to the Accelerated high school

The student's application file is then assessed by a team of educators during a staff meeting to determine if the student meets the eligibility criteria. The team of educators consists of teacher; counselor; and administrator representatives from the traditional high school, the middle school, and the Accelerated high school. If it is decided that the student would benefit from attending the Accelerated high school, his or her file is forwarded to the Student Action Team (SAT).

The Student Action Team, consisting of Accelerated high school students and a teacher, schedules an interview with the prospective student and his or her parent(s) during the Student Action Team scheduled class period. During the interview, the student and parent(s) are given the opportunity to express the reasons they believe the Accelerated high school would best serve the student. The Student Action Team members are given an opportunity to ask questions, discuss expectations, and explain in detail the importance of student and parent commitment to the program.

After the Student Action Team reviews the student application file and interview results, a written recommendation validating their decision is made to the Accelerated school staff regarding the acceptance of the student. The staff makes the final decision concerning the student's acceptance and date of enrollment. The parent(s) and student are notified in writing within 4 school days.

On acceptance, the parent and student commitment contracts are mailed to the student's residence. It is the hope of the Accelerated high school staff that when these documents are received, the student and his/her parent(s) take a close look at the expectations specified. Parents and student are asked to sign the contracts and return them to the school as soon as possible to signify the end of the acceptance procedure. Signatures by all parties help to ensure that the contract will be honored throughout the school year. These commitment contracts, along with a student emergency card and copy of the student's birth certificate, must be on file in the office before the student is able to attend school. (Sample forms and commitment contracts can be found in the Resources section at the end of the book.)

Student Dismissal

As part of establishing an image of a "privilege school," it is necessary to determine *conditions for student dismissal* for students or parents who will not make a commitment to the school and its programs. There are always a few students and parents who may not benefit from the Accelerated high school no matter how much time and effort are given to them by the staff. It may become necessary to dismiss these students from the alternative school for the well-being of the other students, parents, and staff members.

The planning team uses the inquiry process to determine the conditions for student dismissal. We urge each school district planning team to develop a list of conditions for student dismissal that describes the specific situations of the students in their alternative school. Below is an example of specific situations in which students in our Accelerated high school may be dismissed:

Conditions for Student Dismissal

- Excessive nonparticipation and nonattendance during Community Service projects and off-site experiences
- Excessive Student Action Team referrals and nonachievement of behavioral action plan goals
- Excessive unacceptable attendance habits, including tardiness
- Not progressing academically due to lack of effort after two semesters
- Excessive and continuous incomplete assignments
- Continuous disruptive behavior in unstructured time
- Excessively negative attitude toward school program, staff, or other students
- Excessive lack of respect to adults and other students, as well as school property
- Lack of commitment and support by parents to help child be responsible and successful
- Unwillingness to accept change as school evolves
- Excessive disregard of school rules

When the rules and conditions are specifically spelled out for at-risk students, the responsibility becomes totally theirs to accept or reject. At-risk students typically come to the alternative school with no desire to take responsibility for their actions and typically have parents who enable them to be irresponsible. Because the Accelerated high school is a "Privilege School," the students must *earn* the right to attend this school to really internalize the honor of this privilege. It only takes the dismissal of a few students before the other students and parents take their commitment contracts seriously.

Total School Population, Grade Span, and Class Size

A review of literature suggests alternative schools should have a small total student population. It appears that most successful alternative schools have 100 to 300 students, which allows the staff to give more personal academic and social attention to each at-risk student (Glasser, 1969; Kellmayer, 1995; NASSP & Carnegie Foundation, 1996). A small student population allows at-risk students to know every student and staff member in the school. Student-teacher relationships are easier to develop and strengthen when there are fewer students to compete against for attention. Feelings of alienation and crowdedness are diminished in smaller schools. There is also more time for teachers to give one-on-one academic tutoring to students and time for one-on-one exploration and in-depth study of topics.

Grade Spans to Consider

We advocate serving grades 8 through 12 because many eighth-grade at-risk students are older than their classmates because of previous retentions. According to interviews held with students at the Community School, at-risk students seem to contemplate dropping out of school while they are in eighth grade. This coincides with findings in the literature. Educators need to turn students' thoughts away from dropping out and help at-risk students set goals and plans for graduating from high school. We have found eighth grade to be an optimal time to reverse thoughts of dropping out, especially if the eighth-grade students can catch up to their original class through ninth-grade makeup lab independent study courses. In the Accelerated high school, students can make up lost credits through independent study labs with an assigned teacher. The students take the independent study courses through computer courses supplemented with hands-on projects. A paraprofessional monitors the students in the labs. The assigned certified teacher and the students meet a few times per week to check on progress or work on specific projects.

Class Size

Students who are at risk for school failure and have a potential for dropping out of school need to be in small, heterogeneous classes of no more than 10 to 15 students. In small classes, there are fewer opportunities for students to "fade into the woodwork." Opting out of participating in class discussions or group activities is not an option. The teacher is able to spend more one-on-one time and attention with his or her students when the class size is 15 or below. Small class size also gives the students and teacher extra time to develop strong bonds and relationships while talking or doing projects together. The teacher has time to be more of a facilitator of learning instead of the director of learning.

At-risk students tend to "fade into the woodwork" in large homogeneous classes at the traditional high school. Due to the feelings of alienation, depression, frustration, boredom, or apathy, many at-risk students are perfectly content to sit in the back of the classroom, rarely joining in the class discussions or asking questions of the teacher. It is easy to go unnoticed in a class of 25 to 30 students when the teacher teaches five to six classes each day with 25 to 30 students in each class. Many at-risk students in that situation become masters at acting invisible, not causing problems, not participating, and not learning.

Other at-risk students become so frustrated and anxious in classes of 25 to 30 students that they act out, becoming verbally and sometimes physically aggressive or disruptive. They often find themselves in the principal's office or in-school suspension rooms, missing vital instruction and interactions with classmates. Many young people who exhibit such acting-out behavior end up in special education behavioral disorder programs or out-of-school suspensions for extended periods of time.

Facilities and Grounds

Determining the facilities and grounds needed to house the Accelerated high school is a very important aspect of the overall plan. Some school districts allocate several classrooms or a wing of the traditional high school to house their alternative school. This setup is not very conducive to raising the self-esteem of the at-risk students enrolled in the alternative school. Observations and discussions with students attending alternative programs in the traditional high school buildings reveal that these students feel negatively labeled and stigmatized by peers and teachers in the regular classes. The at-risk students feel they are "not as good" as the students in the rest of the building.

We advocate utilizing a separate school building or facility away from the traditional high school campus if possible. In this way, the students, staff, parents, and community members have the opportunity to create their dream school from its inception. A separate off-campus facility enables the stakeholders to take ownership in and develop pride and respect for their school. It is easier for the students, staff, parents, and community to view the Accelerated high school as a "Privilege School" when it has its own building and grounds.

When the Accelerated high school is in a separate building, the students and staff can make it into "their" school with its own motto, song, logo, and personality. Procedures and policies can be developed specifically for and by the stakeholders involved with the alternative school. The school climate and vision will reflect the values, beliefs, attitudes, and needs of the people affected by the school.

The Accelerated high school should be deliberately differentiated from the traditional high school in every way, even in the decor and physical layout of the building. Many at-risk students come from lower-socioeconomic-level households and dysfunctional families in which their physical home lacks comforts, and the atmosphere is less than nurturing and loving. The Accelerated high school provides a warm, accepting, family-like atmosphere that includes the building looking like a home instead of an institution. We advocate such things as installing carpet on the floors and wallpaper or murals on the walls; silk or real flowers in the classrooms; and pictures of students, staff, parents, and community members around the school building.

The classrooms should be warm, colorful, and informal to put the students and staff at ease. The walls should be covered with student work to instill pride and motivation in the students. Small classrooms and large classrooms should be decorated as intimate "gathering rooms." There needs to be computer labs, with sections of the room reserved for individual or small group project work space.

The grounds should look inviting and clean and show a personal touch from the students and staff. The adult stakeholders can participate in powerful learning experiences by helping the students build benches and tables for outside gathering places or classes. Planter boxes and flower beds help make the school look more like a home, with a relaxed, informal atmosphere.

Resources Needed to Start the School

When starting an alternative school from scratch, there are many things that need to be obtained to ensure a successful first year of operation. The planning team should use the inquiry process to determine the resources that are needed to open the Accelerated high school and add to the family-like atmosphere while adhering to the focus of the school. The following is a sample list of start-up furniture, equipment, materials, and supplies that help make the Accelerated high school motivating and inviting to at-risk students and their parents:

- Couches, conference tables, chairs, lamps, and bookshelves to make each classroom look like a living room in a home
- Computers, laser disks, videos, software, satellite dish, camcorders, VCRs, overhead projectors, and interactive technology to engage students in active and powerful learning experiences

- Reference books, magazines, journals, and newspapers for research projects
- A variety of art materials for formal art classes and for student projects within core subjects (A kiln for ceramics is a wonderful asset to provide powerful learning experiences for at-risk students.)
- Office equipment and supplies
- Intercom system and security system
- Equipment, materials, and supplies for the students to perform Community Service Learning projects throughout the school year
- Round tables, seating six to eight students for an informal "cafe" look in the student cafeteria
- Paper, pencils, and other standard school supplies for students and staff

The Grading System

Observations and staff interviews at the Meramec Valley Community School in Pacific, Missouri, along with a review of the literature, find at-risk students unmotivated to academically achieve up to their true potential. After years of frustration, retentions, and self-esteem battering, these students virtually give up by the seventh or eighth grade. By this time, they have learned that if they make a D in their schoolwork, the teachers and their parents will leave them alone.

In an Accelerated alternative School, D work is unacceptable as it does not teach at-risk youth to utilize their strengths and talents. D work does not teach them that employers will not tolerate minimum effort from employees and a D is in reality a minimum effort. To combat this D mentality in at-risk youth, the "A, B, C, Incomplete" grading system has been implemented at the Community School and has been quite effective.

In our experiences with at-risk students, we find that they are very content with making a D grade even though the majority of the at-risk students have the capabilities to make As and Bs. In the Accelerated high school, students are not given the option of making just a D. There are no Ds or Fs in the grading system. A student at the Accelerated high school can only make grades of A, B, C, or Incomplete. The As, Bs, and Cs are based on the same percentages as the entire school district grading scale. Students must complete C-quality work or better on all assignments, tests, and authentic assessments to pass the course. If any grade is below C level at the end of the quarter or semester, the grade of Incomplete is recorded on the student's report card. The student then has until a specified date, usually at the end of the school year, to work independently and raise that grade to a C or better.

If the student does not meet C or better or fails to complete the assignments by the specified date, the course is erased from the student's transcript. The student then has to take the course over the next semester. The lesson here is an obvious one; many at-risk students have difficulty following through with commitments. Therefore, to receive credit for a course, the student must show a commitment by maintaining a minimum C-level work throughout the entire course of study in each subject or is required to start over from the beginning. The lesson to be learned is, "There will be no enablement by the staff to allow the students to do mediocre work when they have the intelligence to produce beyond the C level."

Since 1995, when the A, B, C, Incomplete grading system was implemented, failure rates in courses have dropped by 62%. Students appear excited about their grades and the credits they have earned. Teachers report higher-quality projects and presentations being produced by their students. A majority of parents indicate approval for this grading system on the End-of-the-Year Parent Survey. Seventy-eight percent of our students made the honor roll during the 1996-1997 school year.

At-risk students can excel when enablement and low expectations are absent from parents and teachers. By drawing the line in the sand and telling our students, "Ds are not good enough for you!" we have seen a remarkable rise in their self-esteem, pride and responsibility for their learning process, and performance level. Self-pride is evidenced by a 16-year-old student who told the office secretary, "Since I can't get by with just turning in any old thing for a D, I really started doing the assignments correctly. I made all Bs on my report card and I'm putting it on the refrigerator at home! My mom will just croak!"

Attendance Policy and Credits

Regular attendance is a major problem area for at-risk students. School is not a priority in their young lives; therefore, many at-risk students come to school mainly for the social interactions with friends, not to get an education. At-risk students find themselves losing high school credits due to lack of regular attendance. Each time they lose a credit, it puts them further behind their original graduation date. We find students dropping out of school as they realize they are 1 to 2 years off track for graduating with their original classmates.

The Accelerated high school provides a strict attendance policy to help its at-risk population learn responsibility and commitment to themselves, the staff, their classmates, and the school. The following is an example of an attendance policy that specifically spells out the expectations about student attendance and the consequences if the expectations are not met:

Sample Attendance Policy

Each student at the Accelerated High School must complete a minimum of seven semesters of school and earn a minimum of 24 high school credits to qualify for graduation. Most students usually complete eight semesters of high school and earn 24 to 28 credits before receiving their high school diploma.

Because the Accelerated High School uses the quarter system and each 90-minute course equals one half credit, the attendance policy is as follows:

Tardies:	Four (4) unexcused Tardies equals one absence.
Absences:	Six (6) unexcused Absences from this school per quarter results in loss of all credits for the quarter the six absences occurred.
	After six (6) absences, either excused or unexcused, a student must have a doctor's note.
	After a combination of excused and unexcused absences that equal eight (8) absent days per quarter, the student will lose credit for the quarter.

Regaining Lost Credits

It is unrealistic to think that at-risk students will make an abrupt about-face and start coming to school each and every day after years of irregular and low attendance. Many of these students start every quarter with good intentions but fall back into old habits as the quarter draws on, especially in the last few weeks of the quarter. To meet the needs of these students and allow them to continue to work on breaking their low attendance habit, the Accelerated high school provides a way to regain lost credit and make up lost attendance days.

If a student wishes to regain lost credits, he or she must complete *all* of the following steps:

1. Attend school on time each day for the *remainder* of the school year, unless there is genuine illness preventing school attendance.
2. Any absences must have a doctor's note with a diagnosis and date of office visit.
3. All assignments must be completed at the C level or above and turned in to the teachers.
4. Student must participate in all class discussions, school activities, and projects, including Community Service.
5. Student must attend Evening School to make up lost attendance and assignments. The number of days required to attend Evening School is determined by the number of days absent. Five Evening School sessions equals 1 1/2 days of regular school.

Evening School

Evening School is an integral part of the Accelerated high school as another support for the at-risk student population. Evening School is provided five nights per week from 2:30 p.m. (when day school lets out) until 5:00 p.m. Students are monitored by a teacher and a paraprofessional in the computer labs. Students are encouraged to use this time to complete assignments they missed during their absence or have fallen behind in during class time. The teacher and paraprofessional are available to tutor students and help in any way needed.

Evening School is also used for an alternative to in-school suspensions. It is the belief of the Accelerated high school that in-school suspension during regular school hours is a waste of time. Students assigned to daytime in-school suspension miss vital class instruction and positive social and intellectual interactions with their classmates. Students who have not met their goals in their behavior action plan may be assigned a specific number of sessions in Evening School by the Student Action Team. Again, students assigned to Evening School as an alternative to daytime in-school suspension are given the opportunity for one-on-one help by the teacher and paraprofessional on duty.

Students may voluntarily sign up for Evening School if they want extra teacher help in a subject or if they are behind on assignments. We have found that many at-risk students voluntarily take advantage of Evening School to catch up on assignments or projects, as indicated by daily attendance sheets in the Evening School labs. We find Evening School labs average 12 to 15 students per day.

The Daily Schedule

The daily schedule is an extremely important aspect of the Accelerated high school. We have found a correlation between the daily schedule of courses and the motivation and performance level of at-risk students. This information helped the staff, students, and parents develop a daily schedule that fit the needs of students and staff better than a traditional 7- or 8-class-hour day. Through interviews with students enrolled at the Community School and at-risk students on the Community School's waiting list, we learned that the traditional high school's seven to eight courses per day are very frustrating and unmotivating for these students.

Typically, at-risk students do not complete homework and have attendance problems, thereby keeping them perpetually behind in each of their courses. It becomes a vicious cycle for these teenagers to catch up with their classes. They soon become overwhelmed by the amount of work that has to be completed to receive high school credit for each course. Many at-risk students simply give up, quit school, do just enough to get by, or stay in high school five to six years if they have parents who do not allow them to quit school.

Block Scheduling

We found that *block scheduling* is very effective in motivating and easing academic stress for at-risk students and their staff. Block scheduling allows students and teachers to become involved in more in-depth and challenging studies in their subjects due to the increase of instructional time from 45 minutes to 90 minutes per class period. Teachers have fewer students in their daily caseload, thereby enabling them to spend more time with each student and utilize a variety of instructional techniques during the longer class time. The longer class periods enable teachers and students to bond quickly and have more time to get to know each other as "real people." According to a review of the literature, increasing time is critical to increasing achievement and understanding (McGowan, 1972; Powell, 1976).

Many types of block scheduling are being utilized in middle schools and high schools across America today. The type of block schedule chosen should be based on having enough staff to implement it successfully and the needs of the students who will be impacted by it. For example, through the staff and students we interviewed at the Community School, we learned that both the teachers and students did not want to study seven to eight separate subjects each week. They indicated they would prefer studying three to four subjects per quarter and receive a half credit for each 90-minute course. The students and staff preferred to change courses each quarter to decrease boredom and frustration on both their parts.

The problem to solve in trying to honor the wishes of the students and staff became how to develop this type of block schedule and allow students to be able to have seven to eight courses by the end of each semester in case they wanted to transfer back to the traditional high school or if they moved to a different school district. The staff and students decided that first- and third-quarter courses would be the same and that second- and fourth-quarter classes would be the same. In this type of block scheduling, students transferring in or out of the Community School could easily fit into a traditional seven- or eight-period day at a traditional high school without losing credits. An example of this type of block scheduling is provided in Figure 6.1.

The data gathered over the past 3 years indicate the staff and students like this type of daily schedule. Attendance rates have increased from 79% in 1994 to 92% in 1997 due in large part to the students realizing they have courses for only 9 weeks at a time. Staff members report less student "burnout" and frustration because the students know they are changing courses each quarter. Staff members

Student Schedule

Student Name:	Jim Thomas	Family: Mrs. Smith		Grade: 9
Time:	1st Quarter	2nd Quarter	3rd Quarter	4th Quarter
7:20-8:55	American History	Biology	American History	Biology
8:55-10:25	English 9	Pre-Algebra	English 9	Pre-Algebra
10:25-10:45	Family Time	Family Time	Family Time	Family Time
10:45-11:30	Community Service	Community Service	Community Service	Community Service
11:30-12:00	Lunch	Lunch	Lunch	Lunch
12:00-1:30	Physical Education	Crafts	Physical Education	Ceramics
1:30-2:20	Health	Health	Health	Health

Figure 6.1. Block Scheduling
NOTE: Total credits possible to earn this school year: 8

also report that they do not feel as stressed or overwhelmed because they have the lower student caseload. They indicate they enjoy getting to spend more time with their students during the 90-minute classes. Teachers and paraprofessionals report more time for class discussions, working on projects, helping students one-on-one, and group work and less tension in the classrooms to "get things done in a hurry."

Program Evaluation and Revision

Every successful school or program undertakes *program evaluation activities* to measure the outcomes of its goals and progress toward achieving its vision. It is extremely important for the Accelerated high school stakeholders to conduct continuous program evaluation activities to ensure that the academic, emotional, and social needs of the at-risk students are being met effectively. Continuous program evaluation activities should also be conducted to ensure that the Accelerated Schools philosophy and process are being adhered to properly as the stakeholders work together to create their dream school.

Another reason for continuous program evaluation activities is that alternative schools are constantly under the scrutinizing eyes of traditional educators, parents, the community, state departments of education, and state and federal legislatures. Alternative schools are "under the gun" to show positive results in academic achievement, lower dropout rates, decreased discipline problems, and increased social responsibility in at-risk students. It is only through using a variety of data collection methods that an alternative school can look at the whole picture and judge the effectiveness and success of its program with regard to the at-risk student population it serves. Continuous assessment or evaluation gives the stakeholders the data needed to determine if the program goals have been met, are progressing, or need to be revised to achieve the Accelerated high school's vision.

We advocate conducting program evaluation through the utilization of a variety of methods to obtain as much unbiased and valid data as possible. Assessing for program effectiveness is the process of observing, studying, recording, comparing, and analyzing information, procedures, policies, achievement, instructional and discipline techniques and methods, curriculum, and climate with regard to the vision's "Where we want to be."

The inquiry process is then used to determine solutions to problems or necessary revisions. Assessment activities should always be compatible with and relevant to the goals, objectives, and content of the Accelerated high school's program. The assessment activities should provide useful information to the stakeholders and result in benefits to the at-risk students with regard to needed revisions to meet the needs and expectations of the students, parents, staff, and community. Continuous program evaluation involves observing the vision at work in the daily life of the school. All the stakeholders should be encouraged to actively participate in the assessment activities in order to obtain a comprehensive diagnosis of the school's progress in achieving its vision.

Questions to Ask When Choosing Assessment Procedures

The following questions adapted from the National Association for the Education of Young Children and the National Association of Early Childhood Specialists in State Departments of Education (NAEYC & NAECS/SDE, 1991, p. 4) may be used as guidelines to ensure that the assessment procedures chosen by the stakeholders can provide the desired information and data:

- Are the assessment activities or procedures based on the goals and objectives of the Accelerated high school's vision?
- Can the results of the assessment activities be used to benefit at-risk students?
- Can the assessment procedures provide useful information to the stakeholders to help them revise the program if necessary?
- Can the assessment procedures obtain demonstrated performance expectations of student achievement or the daily life in the school?
- Can the assessment procedures or activities reflect the individual and cultural differences in the students and other stakeholders in order to obtain unbiased data?
- Can the assessment activities involve collaboration among staff, students, and parents?
- Is there a regular procedure for communicating the results of the assessment activities to all the stakeholders?
- Can the assessment procedures address all the components of the delivery of the program?

Effective Program Evaluation Activities

Continuous program evaluation should include both quantitative and qualitative assessment activities. By utilizing both types of assessment tools, the stakeholders can obtain rich descriptions and statistics about the Accelerated high school's effectiveness at keeping at-risk students in school and motivated to learn. The following are some examples of good assessment activities that give a variety of information and data with which to analyze the effectiveness of the program:

Short-range comparison studies are very effective for determining if the attendance rates for the at-risk students enrolled in the Accelerated high school have increased as compared to their attendance rates when they were enrolled at the traditional high school. Comparison studies can also be conducted to determine if the at-risk students are more motivated to earn credits since enrolling at the Accelerated high school as compared to the number of credits earned when they were enrolled at the traditional high school. Comparison studies can be conducted on other program components, such as dropout rates from year to year at the Accelerated high school, out-of-school suspensions, student grades, discipline referrals, and increase in students' self-esteem. Comparison studies of this nature utilize information about individual students but can be reported in group percentages; for example, 90% of the at-risk students earned 6.5 credits during the 1996-1997 school year at the Accelerated high school as compared to the 4.5 credits this same group earned at the traditional high school during the 1995-1996 school year.

Tracking graduates is another assessment activity that gives information on how well the Accelerated high school prepares its students for life after high school. We advocate keeping records of the number of graduates who go on to a junior college, 4-year college or university, vocational-technical postsecondary school, the military, apprenticeships with labor unions, or full-time employment, as well as the number unemployed.

Standardized achievement test scores can also be utilized in the assessment procedures for program evaluation. We recommend not putting a heavy emphasis or weight on standardized test scores with regard to at-risk students, however. This form of testing is not compatible with the cognitive learning style of many at-risk students. These students have grown up taking these types of tests year after year in the traditional school without showing much academic progress from year to year.

In our observations of at-risk students taking standardized achievement tests, we have seen students fill in the circles quickly and indiscriminately; fill in the circles to make a flower design on their test sheet, leaving the rest of the test blank; and mark circles and finish the 50-minute test in 10 minutes, to name a few behaviors as examples. At-risk students may have a horrendous evening with their family the night before the tests are to be given and the last thing these teenagers want to do when they get to school with their emotions undone is sit down and take a fill-in-circles test. In discussions with at-risk students, we learned that many at-risk students do not take these tests seriously because many of the test items are concerned with content they have not been exposed to because they were in remedial, basic skills, or vocational classes at the traditional high school. Hence, the flower designs made of filled-in circles on the student answer sheets!

End-of-the-year program evaluation surveys for parents and students give some good information, but it can be difficult to get the parents to return a completed survey. If the survey is to be completed anonymously, the data may or may not reflect the true feelings of the people filling it out. Sometimes, disgruntled parents will bias the survey because they displace their feelings at a teacher or the principal instead of the program. We recommend that surveys be developed to answer specific questions about the school and its program that can elicit data that can benefit the students. Make sure there are no questions in which parents or students can personally attack specific teachers, the principal, or other staff members, as that is not the purpose of this type of assessment activity. A copy of sample end-of-the-year program evaluation forms for parents and students can be found in the Resources section. We recommend that Accelerated high schools develop their own surveys, using parts of the sample surveys if desired, in order to obtain data that is relevant to their students and parents.

Authentic assessment activities bring an abundant amount of qualitative data that are extremely important in determining the school's progress in achieving the vision. Authentic assessment activities take place during the daily happenings at the school. Rich, descriptive information can be gathered through the following authentic assessment activities:

- Interviews with students, parents, staff, central office administrators, school board members, and community members
- Keeping an Accelerated high school scrapbook of all the events and work during the Accelerated Schools process each year (Include newspaper articles about the alternative school, visitors lists, awards, and honors)
- Stakeholders' written observations of the various aspects of the school and its program
- Teacher observations and anecdotal records on student achievement, behavior, and social responsibility
- Student and staff reflection papers with regard to the school's progress in becoming an Accelerated high school and achieving the vision
- "Fireside chats" between small groups of students and the principal to discuss "What is working and what is not" with regard to the school policies, procedures, instructional techniques, etc.

Revising Aspects of the Program

The name of the game with regard to an alternative school is constant change. As the students, staff, parents, and community members come to really know and trust each other and know the needs, values, beliefs, and attitudes of each group, a unity of purpose emerges and change is seen as good and necessary among the stakeholders. As the assessment data are gathered and analyzed, the stakeholders may find some changes need to be made to keep the Accelerated high school moving toward achieving the vision. When alternative schools are started, changes are made almost continuously throughout the first few years. An effective and successful alternative school continues to evolve and change as long as it remains in existence.

The Accelerated high school as an alternative school is developed and implemented for students at risk for school failure and dropping out. Each year new at-risk students are accepted into the school who may bring specific academic, social, emotional, and physical needs that require changes to be made in the school's program in order to meet those needs. All the Accelerated high school stakeholders, especially the staff, must be flexible and open to change when necessary.

If possible, we recommend holding staff meetings three to four times per week for 30- to 40-minute sessions to continuously evaluate or revise daily procedures or discuss student needs and progress. Creativity is needed to schedule a meeting time for the entire staff three to four times per week. For example, the Community School staff members decided to exercise flexibility in their schedule because they feel the daily staff meetings are vital to the success of the Accelerated high school. The school district's teacher contract requires teachers to be in their classrooms 30 minutes before school starts and 30 minutes after school lets out. The Community School staff members opted to be in their classrooms 15 minutes before school starts and hold staff meetings for 45 minutes four times per week after school.

The staff meetings are invaluable for creating a true atmosphere of comradeship and support among the staff. Procedures and policies are discussed and recommendations for changes are forwarded to the appropriate cadre to consider. Staff members share ideas on a multitude of subjects and build a unity of purpose, become empowered with responsibility, and build on each other's strengths during the meeting time. Blank agenda forms are available for staff members to fill in a topic or topics they feel need to be addressed at the day's meeting. Agenda topics must be turned in to the office by 1:30 p.m. if the topic or topics are to be discussed that afternoon at the staff meeting. This gives the principal and other staff members time prior to that day's meeting to gather any needed information about the topics to be discussed.

Chapter Summary

To move from the taking stock stage to achieving the Accelerated high school's vision, the planning team must set priorities for the stakeholders to implement in order to achieve the vision and create their dream school. The planning team begins the fashioning to get the Accelerated high school started and then turns it over to the cadres to do the expanding, detailing, and refining of the various components discussed in this chapter.

Each aspect of the Accelerated high school utilizes the inquiry process to find solutions to the challenges before the planning team and stakeholders to achieve the vision of the alternative school. All the plans for the school's policies, procedures, and daily operations need to be based on sound educational research and the needs of the specific types of at-risk students to be served. Once the planning team decides on the at-risk students to be served, the rest of the planning should be focused on making the Accelerated high school deliberately differentiated from the traditional high school in order for the at-risk students to succeed and ultimately graduate.

Once the basic day-to-day operations are in place, it becomes time to reflect on ways to provide continuous program evaluation and assessment to determine how well the school is progressing toward achieving its vision. Effective and successful alternative schools conduct continuous program evaluation and revise their programs or procedures to meet the academic, social, emotional, and physical needs of the at-risk student population they serve. It is important for all stakeholders to be encouraged and provided with opportunities to actively participate in assessment activities in order to obtain a variety of data and be able to make a comprehensive diagnosis of the progress of the school. The inquiry process is utilized to determine the solutions to any problems found in the program evaluation activities and make revisions as necessary.

After the Accelerated high school has fashioned and set the priorities of the school, it becomes necessary to examine instructional techniques that are effective in motivating at-risk students to "turn on" to learning. The inquiry process is quite useful in helping to determine specific instructional techniques and strategies that are compatible with a variety of cognitive learning styles. It can be quite a challenge to get at-risk students motivated to learn and stay in school given the social barriers and issues that many of these teenagers face daily in their young lives. Chapter 7 discusses just such topics.

7

Triumphing Over Barriers
to Academic Achievement

"Learning is not attained by chance. It must be sought
for with ardor and attended to with diligence."

Abigail Adams (1744-1818)
(Petras & Petras, 1995, p. 158)

In an Accelerated alternative school, teachers work as a team, facilitating and developing a family and a community of active learners. Teaching strategies and techniques for at-risk students must be deliberately differentiated from those used in the traditional school. These students do not find success or motivation with the traditional lecture style and passive learning strategies that are used in the traditional school setting.

This chapter discusses a variety of proven strategies, utilizing the Accelerated Schools principles that are effective in helping at-risk students achieve academic success and a motivation to learn even after graduation from high school. Before deciding on actual strategies and techniques to use with these students, teachers must understand and have knowledge of the social issues and barriers along with the characteristics of these students that may interfere with academic learning and appropriate social skills. Educators of at-risk students need to understand that academic and social skills must be linked to connect students' lives to their family, school, community, and the world.

Impact of Social Issues
and Barriers to Learning

Through examining the educational records of identified at-risk students, educators can see that academic learning and emotional and social growth stop when children and adolescents experience areas in their lives that are dysfunctional. Children are not born with an "at-risk gene," but rather life situations and circumstances cause children and adolescents to become at risk for school failure. According to Jim Cummins (1992, p. 7), there are no quick fixes or easy formulas for changing students' lives or circumstances to motivate them to want to learn and achieve. It takes teachers, administrators, counselors, and the rest of the school staff practicing patience, using ingenuity, and showing a genuine spirit of commitment to their students and the school community.

We find in our travels that teachers working in an alternative school generally have a classroom of students who are trying to cope with one or more of the following social issues that impact their academic progress:

Dysfunctional family life is common, with one or both parents abusing alcohol or drugs and exhibiting depression, rage, or violent abusive behaviors. In many dysfunctional families, the custodial parent has a history of abusive and violent live-in boyfriends or girlfriends. Studies indicate depression, poor parenting skills, financial problems, lack of outside support system, and having many children are major contributors to the dysfunction of the family unit. Parents in these families spend so much energy on other problems they have little or no time for their children's emotional needs. Education is not typically a priority in these families' lives.

Poverty and low-social-class status affect 14.7% of our nation's population (Johnson, Dupuis, Musial, Hall, & Gollnick, 1996). Many families in our community are living in poverty and have two working parents barely making ends meet. These parents are usually high school dropouts and can only find jobs that pay a minimum wage. Financial stress from low-paying jobs and low self-esteem have been found to be at the heart of alcohol and drug abuse in many poverty-level families. The children of these families struggle for basic survival needs of food, clothing, shelter, and parental love and attention.

Teenage drug and alcohol abuse are prevalent among this population of students. Low self-esteem, school failure, peer pressure, and dysfunctional family life contribute to chronic use and abuse of alcohol and drugs by adolescents.

Teen pregnancy affects both the teenage mother and teenage father in many areas of their lives. It is very difficult to cope with a baby's physical and emotional needs along with the financial responsibilities and still be a "normal" teenager in high school. Statistics show that without a supportive family and school, teenage parents are at high risk for dropping out of school before graduating. The main problem we find with our teenage parents is the lack of responsible and dependable baby-sitting for their child so they can attend school regularly.

Gangs and cults are increasing at an alarming rate among our nation's young people. Students with identifiable risk factors for school failure are prime candidates for joining gangs and cults as a substitute for their dysfunctional family. Gang members tend to come from low-income neighborhoods and usually join gangs that are race-specific. Gang members range in age from 9 or 10 years through their 20s.

Children from poverty-stricken communities or neighborhoods have little or no material resources for basic survival. These children have to compete for parental attention, privacy, space, food, and the material possessions they see on television. It is almost a fight for survival through utilizing aggressive behavior. Children and adolescents who join gangs generally mistrust adults and have been forced to become self-reliant for all their needs (Jankowski, 1991).

The gangs recruit these vulnerable children and adolescents on the pretense of "taking care of them." The young gang recruits soon look on the gang as their family. They take pride in the outrageous gang behavior and activities.

Acts of delinquency and youth violence are rising in large numbers each day in our country. Students participating in acts of delinquency or violence have little or no family bonds or support system. These youth have been rejected by their parents from an early age, resulting in feelings of alienation, isolation, and hope-lessness. Often, these feelings turn into anger, rage, and ultimately violence di-rected at the family, school, and community.

Although delinquency and violent behavior are most prominent among youth living in poverty, wealthy youth are not immune to this lifestyle and its problems. Delinquent youth from wealthy families feel just as alienated, rejected, and emo-tionally starved as delinquent youth from middle-class and lower-class families. The common thread connecting these groups is the dysfunction of the family. Wealthy parents and lower-socioeconomic-status parents of delinquent youth are frequently found to give little or no loving, positive support to their children. They do not talk together, eat together, or participate in vacations or leisure time together as a family. We can find in the story of Sarah, a student one of us (Carrie Eidson) encountered at the Community school, many contributing factors to Sarah's delinquent behavior.

Sixteen-year-old Sarah is a physically beautiful, wild spirit with a fake self-assur-ance and tough demeanor. Sarah lives with her professional parents and two younger siblings in a wealthy part of the community. She has an IQ of 128 and participated in the district Gifted Program throughout her elementary school and middle school years. Sarah enjoys all the comforts her parents' money buys, yet she is the saddest child I have ever seen.

When Sarah started high school, she abandoned her childhood friends and took up with a wild crowd, taking drugs and vandalizing the community. This crowd of young people practices witchcraft and heavily participates in occult beliefs and practices. Sarah's parents had no clue as to their daughter's "other life" until she was continuously truant from school and arrested for possession of cocaine.

Sarah's parents had not really paid attention to the facts that Sarah had changed her friends; her grades went from As and Bs to Ds; and she constantly dressed in black, with black lipstick and black fingernail polish. Her parents just shrugged off these changes as an "innocent stage she was going through." They admitted to being a little disturbed when Sarah dyed her natural red hair to coal black but never said a word to their daughter about their feelings. Sarah's parents did not notice these changes in their daughter because they were too caught up in their work, dinner parties, and vacations without their children.

By the time Sarah was arrested for possession of cocaine and vandalism, she was failing her classes and starting to exhibit self-mutilating behaviors. These behaviors included using a safety pin to carve a Satanic pentagram into her fore-arm and burning her other arm with cigarettes. Sarah's parents did not under-stand their daughter's behavior and had Sarah admitted to a drug rehabilitation center. On release from the center, Sarah entered our school this past fall.

Like the other new students at the Community School, Sarah was defiant, sullen, negative, and resistant to staff overtures of acceptance and concern dur-ing the first month. Toward the end of September, Sarah marched defiantly into my office, looking like a professional mourner with her black hair, lipstick, fin-gernail polish, and clothes. She put both hands on my desk and leaned over to within inches of my face.

"This school is stupid!" She emphatically told me with a look of total rage.

"Could you be more specific and give me some examples, Sarah?" I calmly asked with a concerned tone of voice as I moved from behind my desk to one of the rocking chairs in my office. I motioned for Sarah to sit in the other rocking chair, but she remained standing by my desk with her arms crossed tightly across her chest. I quietly rocked, giving her time to calm down and tell me what problem brought her to my office.

"This is a school of freaks!" Sarah exploded with frustration and started pacing back and forth, "Your staff is like being with 12 Glendas the Good Witch of the North in the *Wizard of Oz*. They act so concerned and happy. They joke around and laugh with the kids like they mean it. What a joke!"

"The staff is genuine. They are concerned and they enjoy joking and laughing with the kids. Sarah, we're building a family and a community at this school. We've discussed you, Sarah, and we feel that you would be a great asset to our school family if you'd allow yourself to get to know the staff and students." I watched Sarah struggle with her emotions as her eyes filled with tears. She had stopped pacing and was staring at the pictures of my own children on the wall.

"Don't you get it? I miss my old friends. . . they are my family!" Sarah's voice grew loud and emphatic again. "My parents won't allow them to call or let me hang around with them any more. My friends and I are. . . or were a family. They care about me and we can talk about anything. We always did fun and exciting things together."

"Like drugs, vandalism, and occult activities?" I ventured as I observed Sarah starting to relax a bit.

"It was fun and it sealed us together like a family." Sarah now stood next to the other rocking chair. "We were tough and didn't need anybody else. If we didn't want to go to school, we didn't. If we didn't want to go home one night, we didn't. My parents ruined it all by sticking me at this school. The judge told me that if I skip school he will put me in a youth facility. Now my parents are trying to act like we're one big happy family and this is just a 'phase' I'm going through. What geeks! They thought I'd do better at this school, but I'm still flunking all my courses. These teachers and kids are getting on my nerves."

"Are you afraid you might be starting to like this school and the people in it, Sarah?" I asked quietly. Sarah sat in the other rocking chair and looked at the floor.

"What if all this 'family' business at this school is a fake? I'll look like a jerk if I buy it and it's not real."

"You're having a hard time trusting us. Sarah, you've told me that you're tough and you like challenges and taking risks, right? Well, finding out if we're real or not could be the ultimate challenge for you. The risk is that if you find out we're real, you might have to take a hard look at yourself to see if you can let the students and staff get close to you. Are you up to that risk?"

"My parents try to fit me in their schedule and act like I'm the most important thing to them. But they still break promises and cut short family activities. They aren't even honest with our family shrink. I can't see my old friends because of the judge and my probation officer. I feel really alone most of the time," Sarah said quietly, still looking at the floor. "You know, most of the time I can't concentrate on school stuff because of all the other junk in my life. I feel so stressed out and angry all the time."

"I know, Sarah."

"Some of your staff do seem interesting. I kind of like how laid back it is here. . . . If only I knew it's what it seems." Sarah sighed and finally looked at me.

A month has passed since that conversation with Sarah. I notice her smiling a bit. Her hair is still black but the natural red roots are starting to show and her black lipstick has been replaced with a pale red.

Suicide is also an important concern with respect to many teenagers. The rate of teenage suicide in America has tripled in the past 30 years (Johnson et al., 1996). All the issues discussed on the preceding pages are contributing factors to teen suicide. Teachers of at-risk youth are always part counselor, because their students shut down the learning process when they are depressed or suicidal. Major high-risk symptoms of suicide among teenagers include the following:

- Extreme depression causing withdrawal from previous social activities
- Continuous conflicts with one or both parents
- Lack of peer group
- Feelings of alienation and rejection
- Parental divorce
- Moving to a new school
- Breaking up with a boyfriend or girlfriend
- Drug or alcohol abuse
- Deep involvement with occult membership or activities
- Self-mutilation behavior
- Overwhelming stress, loss of appetite, falling grades

As stated before, these social issues place children and adolescents at risk for school failure and eventually contribute to their decision to drop out of school before graduation. Teachers of at-risk youth need to develop a classroom climate and teaching style in which these social issues and barriers are taken into account. The next section discusses instructional techniques effective in motivating at-risk students and keeping them interested in the learning process.

Effective Instructional Techniques for At-Risk Students: Powerful Learning Experiences

Powerful learning experiences are the cornerstone of an effective curriculum for the Accelerated alternative school. A powerful learning environment is an active environment building on strengths and talents of each student. Teachers and administrators in the Accelerated alternative school must collaborate with students, parents, and community to create learning situations that are interesting and can be connected to real-life situations (Hopfenberg et al., 1993).

In creating powerful learning experiences, information, skills, and concepts are integrated into lessons, units, and activities that interest and motivate at-risk students. According to Hopfenberg et al. (1993), "Complex activities are stressed, content is relevant, and children actively discover the curriculum objectives in a safe and caring environment rather than passively going through textbooks and filling out worksheets" (p. 161). Powerful learning experiences are developed around what the students need and want and in the learning modality in which the students' strengths and talents lie. Activities are hands-on, interactive, kinesthetic, reflective, challenging, and very participatory.

The Accelerated Schools philosophy views powerful learning experiences as being a triangle of the following three interrelated dimensions:

1. *What:* The powerful learning experience must define what is to be learned—the specific content, skills, and curriculum—along with the students' beliefs about themselves and their relationship to the world outside of school.
2. *How:* The powerful learning experience must define how the information is to be learned. At-risk students thrive on powerful learning experiences because of the required active participation and hands-on nature of the experiences.

3. *Context:* The context of powerful learning experiences brings together the physical setting, materials, staff, time, and funding to achieve the how and what.

The following examples of powerful learning experiences can be incorporated into units of the entire school curriculum:

- Thematic units integrated across the curriculum
- Learning centers with hands-on activities
- Community Service projects
- Whole Language
- Cooperative learning groups and experiences
- Computers, laser discs, modems
- Manipulatives
- Community resource people to teach students a craft or hobby
- Field trips with study guides or projects related to them
- Students making slides for slide show presentation to show mastery of concepts
- Students making a homeless village while studying the homeless issues
- Students making video productions to show mastery of concepts and skills
- Students producing a student radio show
- Students making a plant laboratory for experiments or selling flowers for special occasions
- Academic trivia tournaments
- Students painting murals on school walls depicting concepts learned or themes
- Students writing, producing, and performing plays
- Students writing individual and class books
- Poetry contest
- Students making board games for authentic assessment of concepts learned

Powerful learning experiences result from creative collaboration between students and teachers to develop activities and authentic assessment projects for various concepts, skills, and knowledge. Many powerful learning experiences just happen due to specific needs, timing, and problems presented by the students.

An example of a powerful learning experience can take place on a field trip to the zoo. The objective of the trip might be to sharpen the students' eyes for detail, observation, and analyzing situations. Each student is given a project guide developed by the entire staff with questions developed from each discipline with regard to the zoo animals. The following are a few examples of the activities that can be included in the project guide:

- Compare and contrast in detail the alligator and the crocodile.
- Observe the pink flamingos. Discuss the dynamics of the group. Describe and discuss the group leader and his or her leadership style. Reflect and compare the flamingos' group behavior, leadership qualities, and leadership style to those of humans.
- Trace the history of the zoo by making a timeline of the expansion, remodeling, and new animal environments projects that have occurred since the original opening date of the zoo.
- Compare and contrast the native habitats of the polar bear, grizzly bear, and black bear at the zoo.
- Observe the monkeys and apes with regard to family dynamics, parenting skills, treatment of their young, and group leadership. Compare and contrast your observations of the monkeys and apes with today's human family.

In summary, powerful learning experiences highly motivate and hold the interest of at-risk students. When students are active participants in challenging and authentic learning experiences, they build connections from information learned to application in real-life situations. In other words, students find a personal purpose for academic learning and gaining knowledge. Through powerful learning experiences, students' self-esteem rises as they use their strengths and talents in a specific learning style that fits their cognitive and affective needs.

Cognitive Learning Styles

Many at-risk students are characterized as being underachievers, unmotivated, slow learners, special education students, marginal, apathetic, poor minority, or dysfunctional in the traditional school setting. In reality, the majority of students at risk for school failure are in the range of above-average to superior intelligence. A significant number of students are labeled "learning disabled" because they are not academically successful in the regular education traditional classroom. These students have great difficulty learning from part to whole, sitting all day, doing individual seat work, and gleaning information from a lecture-style class, whether they are labeled "at risk" or "special education" or both.

According to Waxman et al. (1992), identified at-risk students generally have a distinctive cognitive learning style that could affect their academic progress, depending on the school's instructional methodology. A student's cognitive learning style characterizes his or her perceptions, understandings, judgments, and problem-solving style. Cognitive learning styles are heavily influenced by the student's family values and culture and social issues affecting the student.

A review of the literature suggests students at risk for school failure have a cognitive learning style that is incompatible with the traditional American school system's instructional style. If teachers ignore the cognitive learning styles of their students, academic achievement is not realized. If students in a class have a different cognitive learning style from the specific learning style used in the classroom, these students are at a high risk for academic and behavioral problems because of the incompatibility of cognitive learning styles.

Traditional American schools generally use a cognitive learning style classified as being *field independent*. Thus field-independent students have an academic advantage, as their learning style is more compatible with the traditional American school system's instructional methodologies (Davis & Cochran, 1989). The traditional school system requires students to be able to

- Use the scientific trial-and-error method
- Use analytical thinking skills—especially in science, math, and reading
- Attend to tasks without getting distracted
- Follow a rigid time schedule
- Work well with detailed factual information
- Follow verbal and written directions and instructions
- Do seat work for long periods of time
- Work individually and have a long attention span
- Rely on memorization and drill to build a large knowledge base

In contrast, at-risk students usually have a cognitive learning style classified as *field dependent* (Saracho & Spodek, 1981). Students who have a field-dependent cognitive learning style tend to need the following:

- A structured and organized learning environment
- Social interaction and active participation in the learning process
- Concrete, visual examples to retain information
- Visual rather than verbal instructions
- Opportunities to learn by observing how things are done or occur
- Guidance and examples from adults and other students when learning new methods
- Hands-on learning activities versus passive learning activities

By focusing on the learning strengths of students, teachers can gradually introduce techniques that are not compatible with the students' dominant learning style, thus creating a blend of field-dependent and field-independent strengths (Saracho & Spodek, 1981). Baum, Renzulli, and Hebert (1994) indicate that allowing students to choose topics that personally interest them and show mastery in their own cognitive learning style often results in high achievement.

Multiple Intelligences

The concept of instruction using *multiple intelligences* fits into the philosophy of the Accelerated Schools and Caring Communities like a piece of the puzzle. Multiple intelligences theory defines intelligence as "Seven Ways of Knowing" that provide the ability to solve real-life problems and produce things of value to our culture (Lazear, 1991).

The multiple intelligences can be defined as:

1. *Intrapersonal Intelligence:* Knowing oneself, capacity for self-discipline, self-reflection, awareness of spiritual realities in problem-solving abilities
2. *Interpersonal Intelligence:* Personal relationships, sensitivity to others, and communication ability in problem solving or influencing others
3. *Kinesthetic Intelligence:* Physical movement, wisdom of the body through control by the brain's motor cortex
4. *Verbal/Linguistic Intelligence:* Oral and written language abilities
5. *Musical/Rhythmic Intelligence:* Sensitivity to and recognition of tonal patterns, rhythms, and beats
6. *Logical/Mathematical Intelligence:* The ability to deal with abstract patterns and concepts; inductive and deductive reasoning and thinking
7. *Visual/Spatial Intelligence:* The ability to visualize objects and spatial relationships; visual discrimination

According to Thomas Armstrong (1994), all human beings possess all seven intelligences. The problem lies in the fact that most people have strengths in some intelligences but not in all seven. It should be the task of educators to help all students develop each of their seven intelligences to their full potential. The seven intelligences work together in a variety of ways each day as students explore and discover the world around them. An example of the importance of multiple intelligences is that each must be evaluated for possible handicapping conditions and deficits in the case of a child referred for a special education psychological evaluation. These intelligences are critical to consider when planning programs, curriculum, units, and lessons for students at risk for school failure.

Multiple intelligence instruction can be conducted through such techniques as Whole Language, cooperative learning, Community Service Learning, technology, and challenging curriculum. Developing the multiple intelligences requires teachers to leave behind the textbooks, dittos, lectures, drill, and memorization exercises. Instruction for developing each intelligence requires teachers to provide powerful learning experiences that relate academic information to real-life situations. It requires teachers to be facilitators and mentors to their students as the students actively and purposefully interact with their environment. When using multiple intelligences in the learning process, students become active participants in exploring and discovering new knowledge and solving problems in real-life situations. Multiple intelligences theory is an excellent tool for creating and implementing powerful learning experiences.

Accelerated and Challenging Curriculum

Throughout the history of American education, students at risk for school failure have been assigned to remedial classes, special education classes, low-track classes, vocational education, and functional classes. Assignments to these classes have been and continue to be based on IQ, achievement level, teacher observation, social class, school behavior, motivation, and attitude. In the case of IQ, most at-risk students never receive an individual IQ test or, if they do, no one really looks into the fact that the IQ may be depressed due to family problems, social barriers, or depression from low self-esteem. Even if these at-risk students have the ability for regular or advanced studies, they find themselves in remedial or functional classes based on one or more of the reasons stated above.

Is it any wonder these students are unmotivated, apathetic, sullen, negative, frustrated, and unproductive? Their academic world is full of dittos, workbooks, drill, memorization, books of little interest written for younger children to match their reading level, and crowded classrooms with no role models of average or gifted peers. Students in these classes are bored and usually act in accordance with the self-fulfilling prophecy, "I'm not good enough or smart enough, so why even try?"

If at-risk students are lucky enough to be assigned to a heterogeneous class, they usually end up in low groups or are pulled out of the core subjects to receive "extra help" in the resource room through special education or Title I services. These students miss the class discussions in which they could learn information and new ideas from their average or gifted peers. What motivation or intrinsic rewards do at-risk students receive to continue in school through high school graduation if school is such a boring and self-esteem-killing place?

We need to take a hard look at American education to determine how our schools are failing children by not meeting their specific educational needs (Waxman et al., 1992). Statistics show us that our schools are failing not just our disadvantaged and minority students but also our apathetic gifted students. Their needs are illustrated by the situation of Lucas, another student one of us (Carrie Eidson) encountered at the Community School.

A Place for Lucas

"Hey, lady, you got a nice place here for a school, but this just isn't the place for me. I mean, the teachers won't leave me alone for a minute. They keep trying to get me to discuss stuff and keep asking me my opinion. I just want to glide and fade in the back of the room, you know? I have been here for 3 hours and they all know my name."

The short, skinny, 16-year-old boy sitting next to me spoke quietly and politely.

"Your teachers expect me to do Algebra because they say I'm smart. At my other school, I was in General Math because I never would do the homework so they thought I couldn't do math. Why do you guys around here care so much if I participate or care about what I think? No one else ever has!"

Lucas and I sat in the rocking chairs in my office at the Community School discussing his plight of having so many adults showing interest in him and not allowing him to fade into oblivion in their classrooms. Lucas had never been challenged to interact with his classmates or teachers at the schools he had attended in the past. His high intelligence was hidden from others beneath his detached look of boredom and lack of motivation in the traditional school setting. His referral form stated Lucas was a D and F student.

I looked at this bewildered boy dressed in designer clothes, looking like a model for a prep school ad, and wondered what happened in his life to cause his past teachers to label Lucas as "at risk for school failure." According to the referral form, his other teachers felt Lucas would never stay in school to graduate. What caused Lucas to give up on education or, more precisely, school?

My mind wandered from Lucas to the other 100 at-risk students attending the Community School. They come from all socioeconomic backgrounds and a variety of family makeups. They have different values, ideas, family traditions, dress styles, and personalities. But these students have some things in common, such as above-average intelligence, lack of motivation, lack of success in past school experiences, distrust of adults, lack of responsibility, low self-esteem, and feelings of alienation from school.

The staff and I call these teenagers our "little islands," because when they first come to the Community School, they trust no one and do not allow anyone to get too close to them. We notice immediately that these students do not see the relevance for school in their lives. They cannot get the connection between information learned and applying it to solve problems and issues in their lives. They do not know how to build on experiences to expand their knowledge base.

"Lucas," I ventured, "Why don't you stick around for a week and see if we grow on you? I mean, what's one little week out of your whole life?"

"Well, it's not just school that's been the problem." Lucas spoke quietly, looking down at his hands. I had learned early on that students who are at risk for school failure find it very hard to have eye contact with adults, so I never press the issue. "You see, I been thinking about getting a full-time job so I can move out of my mom's house. If I wait until I can graduate, that would be another 3 years."

"Well, let's take a look at that plan." I let my facial features assume the position of thinking the matter over. "If you quit now with only a ninth-grade education, the best job you could probably get is one that will pay at best only minimum wage. On the other hand, if you stick it out and graduate, you could get a job that might provide better starting wages and benefits. And prospective employers would probably hire you over someone without a diploma who had dropped out of school."

"But I really want my own place," he persisted, "You see, my mom married this idiot last year, and we definitely do not like each other!"

Lucas and I continued to discuss the pros and cons of leaving school and moving out of his mother's house. We explored options and possible solutions. Lucas has been with us now for 4 months. Since our school is a Missouri Accelerated School and a Caring Community, we were able to provide wraparound services to provide Lucas and his family with therapy so Lucas felt comfortable living at home. During these 4 months, we have seen Lucas relax, participate in class discussions, and thrive in Algebra class.

In an Accelerated alternative school, *every* student is treated as if he or she is gifted (Hopfenberg et al., 1993). In these schools, classes are truly heterogeneous, discussions include each student, and the teacher's role is one of being a facilitator of active learning and involvement. Staff, parents, and students have a great deal of input into the curriculum and instructional techniques.

Within the Accelerated Schools philosophy, only challenging and accelerated course work is offered. Because the majority of at-risk students in an alternative school have an average to superior intelligence, remedial work, dittos, workbooks, and passive learning experiences are the "kiss of death" to their self-esteem and academic achievement.

Through continuous student observations; teacher observations; and student, staff, and parent interviews and surveys, we find these students to be excited about learning if they are actively involved in the learning process. Students report they like having choices in how to prove they understand concepts and information. We find at-risk students thriving in classes that are challenging to them and require active participation to solve problems.

To challenge and motivate these students to reach deep inside to tap their real potential and true abilities, they need to be Accelerated throughout the curriculum. For example, if a student has the ability or potential to do well in math but has a track record of putting forth little effort in this area and has been in general math or basic math classes at the traditional school, assign this student to a pre-algebra class to challenge and motivate the student. If information or skill gaps are present due to poor attendance or learning style conflicts from his past school, provide extra conferences, projects, or peer tutoring for the student while he continues in pre-algebra. We find in the majority of cases the student's self-esteem, academic confidence, and motivation to learn rise because the challenging material holds his interest and he has a staff support group that believes in him.

Developing the Accelerated Curriculum

An Accelerated and challenging curriculum for at-risk students must foster the development of cognitive and affective skills. The skills and concepts listed below should be the basis for all curriculums in the Accelerated alternative school. These need to be integrated throughout all subject areas utilizing powerful learning experiences.

- Critical thinking skills
- Problem-solving skills, using the inquiry process
- Brainstorming and consensus building
- Applying new information and concepts to real-life situations
- Developing and implementing action plans
- Analyzing information and testing possible solutions
- Organization skills

- Evaluating social situations and academic projects and problems
- Cooperation among students and staff
- Respect for oneself and others
- Unity of purpose in learning experiences
- Meaningful communication skills (both oral and written)
- Exploring the world around oneself through the five senses
- Giving of oneself to others in the school and community

Constructivist Theory as the Basis for the Accelerated Curriculum

For developing and implementing an Accelerated and challenging curriculum, *Constructivist* theory about knowledge and learning ensures a solid foundation with which to build a community of learners. Constructivism is not a theory of education but serves as a basis for many current reforms in education (Grennon-Brooks & Brooks, 1993). This theory views *knowledge* as subjective, developmental, and stemming from social and cultural interactions. *Learning* is described as being self-regulated and a process that utilizes concrete experiences, collaboration with others, reflections, exploration, and discovery of the world outside the individual. Children's inner cognitive conflicts are resolved through the learning process and shape their understandings.

Traditional American classrooms find the learning process to be teacher-centered and driven instead of student-centered. Students are given textbooks from which they must able to recite the bits of information asked for by the teachers. But there generally is no attempt to help students see the whole picture and connect concepts learned in isolation to real-life situations. Passive learning is the emphasis in these classrooms.

Constructivist teachers help their students to internalize, reshape, and transform new information through the creation of new personal understandings (Jackson, 1986). These teachers utilize the principles of Constructivism to develop challenging learning experiences for their students. As we can see from the list that follows, the principles of Constructivism are the basis of the Accelerated alternative school's instructional philosophy and techniques:

- Students are actively involved in their personal learning process.
- Problem-solving skills emerge as they become relevant to the students.
- Learning is structured around Primary Concepts or the Main Picture.
- The student's point of view is always valued.
- Curriculum is continually being adapted to meet the cognitive needs of the students.
- Student learning is assessed through authentic assessment in the context of teaching. (Grennon-Brooks & Brooks, 1993, p. 34)

Constructivism works quite well with at-risk students, as it gives students more control over their environment and learning process through encouraging and valuing students' active participation in all learning experiences. The teachers provide tasks and projects that center around higher thinking skills such as analyzing, classifying, creating, predicting, and summarizing. This environment allows students to use their specific cognitive learning style. Constructivist teachers utilize instructional techniques such as Whole Language, cooperative learning

experiences, learning centers, projects, and student reflection activities throughout the curriculum activities.

At-risk students flourish in true Constructivist classrooms and schools. Not
only does Constructivist teaching allow the students control over their own learning, it also allows the teachers to be facilitators and partners in the learning process. All learned information is connected to real-life problems and situations.
Constructivism utilizes and requires powerful learning experiences and challenging curriculum. At-risk students work well in cooperative learning groups while
learning the art of collaboration and relationship building. Constructivism encourages and enables at-risk students to build on their strengths and become empowered through having the responsibility for their own learning, and it joins
them in a unity of purpose with their classmates to gain new knowledge and
understandings of the world around them.

Whole Language

Whole Language is a philosophy, a set of beliefs, a perspective, not a practice,
according to Newman's (1985) book *Whole Language: Theory in Use*. Whole Language becomes a practice through methods and strategies developed and used by
the teacher and students. The emphasis is on learning to read, write, speak, and
listen in order to produce meaningful communication to others. Whole Language
is effective with at-risk students because it involves them in active learning experiences at their particular developmental stage (Newman, 1985).

Whole Language advocates using both oral and written language and real
reading such as literature, journals, newspapers, and other print sources for appropriate uses to communicate meaning and build knowledge. Teachers and students use authentic reading material from a vast array of books and other sources,
including:

- Modern fantasy
- Folk tales
- Poems
- Realistic stories
- Mysteries
- Science fiction
- Biographies
- Autobiographies
- Historical fictions
- Comic books
- Recipes
- Cards
- Newspapers
- Magazines

Goodman (1986) indicates schools have traditionally made reading and language arts difficult for children, especially those identified as being at risk, by
breaking language down into parts. Traditional educational thinking has been
based on moving from part to whole. Traditional instructional techniques are
based on the idea that if students learn the small parts of reading and language
first, they can put the parts together to learn the whole reading process. Research

shows, however, that people actually learn from whole to part. Whole Language encourages students to look at the whole to understand the parts and glean the information they are seeking. Students in a Whole Language classroom read a variety of materials because they are motivated to find some information that is important to them personally. Because the students are reading for personal information, they are more likely to extend themselves beyond what they already know.

Teachers utilizing Whole Language do not underestimate the importance of phonics, grammar, or spelling as language tools, but these teachers agree that these skills should be integrated within a meaningful context (Newman, 1985). Writing and reading skills are considered interrelated and inseparable. Studies indicate that student achievement is strongly affected in a positive way when reading and writing skills are taught as integral and connected processes (Goodman, 1986).

Using Whole Language elements with literature-based reading helps stretch students' imaginations while building their knowledge base. For example, folk tales teach cultural differences while showing the universality of humankind. They show each culture's beliefs and customs. Fairy tales conduct moral education and deal with fantastic events. After reading these types of books, students write their own fairy tales and publish individual and class books (Huck, 1977).

By reading literature, young people in at-risk situations learn to feel and identify with characters in the books. Students can feel the sadness of losing a beloved pet, such as in the books, *Where the Red Fern Grows* (Rawls, 1961) and *Old Yeller* (Gipson, 1956). They can identify with the problems and attitudes of the characters in *The Outsiders* (Hinton, 1967) or *To Kill a Mockingbird* (Lee, 1960). Students learn appropriate solutions to problems they read about through class discussions and small group or individual projects. Students reflect and then write about their feelings, ideas, and information learned from their reading.

Thematic units are often used with specific literature chosen to enhance or explain the theme. Activities for the students might include the following:

- Writing their own version of the story they read
- Discussing and writing comparisons between characters in books and people they know
- Discussing the theme and setting
- Making a list of common words used in the book
- Writing and performing live plays from the book
- Making a video of the play performed
- Cooking the food mentioned in the story

Teachers of at-risk students should always use authentic writing in their classrooms. Oral and written language need to be shown as being structurally related to the students. At-risk students need to understand that reading and writing are both meaningful ways of communicating with others. Authentic writing helps these students learn to connect their feelings and knowledge to produce meaningful communication. At-risk students need to feel control in their learning, which the Whole Language writing process allows through student choice in writing on topics that interest and motivate them.

The teacher's role is to nurture the motivation to write by helping at-risk students become aware of what they already know. The teacher is the facilitator, showing the students how to use and share their experiences and interests in writing. As a role model, the teacher shares his or her personal writing with the students. The teacher also responds to the students' writing with personal comments about the subject matter and content.

Assessment of authentic writing is done with *student portfolios*. Students keep a portfolio that includes each piece of writing they do all year. Some pieces are graded and some are not. The teacher and each student confer about the writing pieces, correcting style, grammar, punctuation, and form.

Whole Language is an effective tool for motivating at-risk students to become lifelong readers and writers. It has an important place in the Accelerated alternative school because it fosters the three principles of the Accelerated Schools philosophy while providing active learning experiences for the students. It allows at-risk students some control over what they read and topics to reflect on for writing assignments. Through the Whole Language philosophy, at-risk students receive one-on-one conferences and attention from the teacher. Students explore the world of literature while building their knowledge base and learning more about the world beyond their immediate community. Whole Language also provides the connection between the information the students learn through literature and an application to their real lives through the writing process. Finally, Whole Language is active learning for the students and utilizes the teacher as a facilitator, thereby involving the entire class in the reading and writing process.

Cooperative Learning Experiences

Cooperative learning experiences are effective in helping students at-risk for school failure develop a sense of belonging and personal academic confidence. Cooperative learning is an instructional method that employs small heterogeneous groups collaborating on activities or projects. Each group usually consists of one high achiever, two average achievers, and one low achiever (Slavin, 1987). Group members are charged with helping each other learn the material, skills, or concepts.

This instructional method complements the Accelerated Schools philosophy in that cooperative learning fosters unity of purpose, empowerment with responsibility, and building on strengths. Cooperative learning stresses group collaboration and consensus while working for a common goal or purpose.

In the Accelerated alternative school, cooperative learning groups process and develop *action plans* for each project undertaken. Goals and objectives are developed along with strategies to achieve the action plan goals. Cooperative learning groups must also evaluate their project and the effectiveness of the group's action plan. The teacher is a facilitator, helping and guiding the groups in the development of their action plan. The teacher also plays the role of encourager, cheerleader, and clarifier to make sure all group members are learning the skills or concepts incorporated in the cooperative learning group project.

A component that measures individual group members' understanding and mastery of the skills and concepts should be built into the action plan. Each group member is responsible for his or her own learning and helping group mates understand and learn the information presented through the group project. Each group member is given a specific job to do to help the group achieve the action plan goal or goals. Then, each group member explains the information he or she learned from the specific job assigned and makes sure group mates thoroughly understand it. To check for other group members' understanding, comprehension questions can be developed by each individual member on the information presented. Each student is responsible for checking each group mate's work.

Cooperative learning experiences allow at-risk students to be active and needed participants in a nonthreatening small group. According to Slavin (1987), the success of the group is based on the demonstrated understanding and mastery of the individual group members. With this focus, each member needs to practice acceptance and tolerance of the other members while helping each other master the skills and concepts. Cooperative learning group experiences do not allow at-risk students to "fade into the woodwork" as they generally do in a lecture-style class format.

Instruction Through Technology

A review of the literature and our experiences in the field of the at-risk student indicate that students at risk for school failure need to be actively involved in their journey to gain knowledge and skills for life. We are dealing with a generation of young people who are comfortable with and highly interested in technology. The youth of today are used to the fast-paced, colorful, and intricate problems to be solved on Nintendo, Sega, and computer games. Our nation's young people know how to use computers, software programs, and surf the Internet.

These young people are academically unmotivated from experiencing years of frustration and low self-esteem in passive learning experiences in our schools. Yet, at home, these same youth spend hours upon hours figuring out the problems and solutions to video and computer games. These games provide experiences for developing the following skills:

- Eye-hand coordination
- Fine motor control
- Critical thinking
- Problem solving
- Information analysis
- Visual discrimination
- Observation

Videos and computer games provide ways for students to explore and discover new worlds, old worlds, science, environmental issues, and other subject information.

Technology is a highly effective tool for captivating the interest of and motivating learning in at-risk students. Technology is a needed component in the instructional delivery system of an Accelerated alternative school. Other instructional techniques, such as powerful learning experiences, cooperative learning, Whole Language, and multiple intelligences, are enhanced by the use of technology throughout the curriculum.

According to Gwen Solomon (1993), technology allows all students to tap into multiple intelligences using a different learning style. It encourages and allows at-risk students to feel comfortable and nonthreatened, thereby enabling them to share learning experiences with their partners or small group members. For example, students can design Hypercard stacks for class presentations and write, research, scan, graph, videotape, or develop and produce television broadcasts.

Computers

Computers are a must for the students in an Accelerated alternative school. The most cost-effective and instructionally effective use of computers is to have small computer labs and 5 to 10 computers in each classroom networked through a mainframe server in the building. In this way, students can be in any classroom or computer lab and be able to log on to their personal program or course.

A review of the literature and personal field observations indicate at-risk students are motivated to partake in academic course work on computers. There are many software programs on the market that offer "packaged courses" such as English, Algebra I, General Math, Biology, and so on, but we advocate the software programs that enable the staff to create courses based on their district and state core competency skills. Packaged courses do not allow changing the course objectives and lessons when the school district or state department of education changes the core competency skills. These packaged courses tend to become outdated and expensive to replace as the district and state core competency skills change or become revised.

The software programs that allow the staff to create courses tailored to meet core competency skills may be more expensive initially but more cost-effective over the long haul. Many of these programs can be changed easily to meet new state standards and skills. Teachers can develop new courses by inserting the course objectives, activities, and lessons into the computer. Activities and lessons are usually in binders that come with the programs. The teachers match activities and lessons to the objectives in the various subjects from the binders and create the course. Teachers can develop computer tests with these programs along with teaching aids for the students as they work on the lessons. These software programs generally come with a teacher management section for computer-generated student grades and profiles. Josten's Learning Corporation and Novus have very good software programs of this type.

Tutorsystems is another interactive software system that can be networked throughout the building. This is an effective system with at-risk students, as it first evaluates each student's English, reading, and math skills. After taking the prescriptive tests, the computer designs a specific program in each of the three subject areas for each student. Students work at their own pace and must achieve 90% to 95% mastery on each level before the computer allows them to enter a higher level. This program goes from basic skills to advanced honors in both math and English.

At-risk students especially want and need a variety of interactive software to keep them interested and motivated. Third-party software such as educational and entertainment computer games builds academic skills through the problems the students must solve to win the game. Many games are exploratory, work well with collaborative groupings, require note taking, and utilize critical thinking skills.

Computers as an instructional technique can offer live interactions between students, instructors, scientists, and other resource people across the nation and the world via the Internet and such programs as ones offered by *National Geographic*. In these interactive programs, the students use a fax modem or direct communication on the computer to solve problems or work on projects involving such issues as acid rain, the rain forests, the plight of the homeless, and poverty. It is exciting and motivating for students to be able to communicate live with adults working in the field. This type of instructional use of computers is a very effective and challenging powerful learning experience for at-risk students. It is visual and colorful and involves active participation and critical thinking skills while giving the students some control over their learning.

Videos

Given that today's youth have grown up in the age of videos, it makes sense to utilize this medium in the learning process as an instructional method. According to McKenzie (1992), videos and laser videodisks have proven to be motivating and effective in enhancing the learning process in at-risk students.

Videos should be chosen with regard to their purpose in helping to achieve the academic goals of a lesson or unit. Powerful learning experiences are developed to be used in conjunction with the videos to help the students learn and relate the information or concepts presented to real-life situations. For example, the movie *Mr. Holland's Opus* can be used to demonstrate the following issues:

- The effect on the family of having a disabled child
- Touching people's lives positively without realizing it
- The politics of school finances and priorities
- The role and duties of a teacher
- Teachers' lives outside of school

Educational videos on such topics as gangs, drugs, sports, divorce, and teenage health issues can enhance discussions and impact students' opinions. These videos provide at-risk students with opportunities to extend their learning arena past the school building out into their community or the nation. Teachers need to develop activities to reinforce and allow students to demonstrate understanding of the skills or information presented.

The video camera allows at-risk students to explore another dimension of technology and increase their knowledge. At-risk students usually are not in the classes at the traditional high school that utilize videotaping and production. According to McKenzie (1992), teaching at-risk students to utilize videotaping as a learning tool captures their interest and enhances academic production and artistic skills along with providing feedback for student performance.

At-risk students can write, produce, edit, and perform daily news and announcements, which are then videotaped and shown in each classroom through a networked television station in the school. Our observations indicate that shy, quiet students and students who hate to write willingly write and edit scripts and speak in front of the camera. To be a part of the school news show is quite a self-esteem and confidence builder for these students who would never have the opportunity to participate in such an activity at the traditional school.

Teachers in an Accelerated alternative school constantly encourage their students to use a variety of mediums to solve problems, explore, and discover new information along with demonstrating mastery. Interviews with teachers of at-risk students indicate that more often than not their students choose to make videotapes. Examples of videos the students can make in cooperative learning groups include the following:

- Debates
- Group or class skits and plays

- History of the community through interviews with the elderly in the community
- Murder mystery plays utilizing the students in other grades and the entire staff
- Documentaries for history or science projects
- Acting out nursery rhymes for preschoolers to view
- Research projects

In videotape projects, students use the Accelerated Schools inquiry process to develop their action plan for accomplishing the goals of the project. Everyone in the cooperative learning group is assigned one or more responsibilities in the production of the video. Video projects require the utilization of information and skills across the curriculum. Students must research their topic, write scripts, memorize lines, make backgrounds and costumes, collect props, and set lighting and sound along with editing the tape.

Video production as an instructional technique utilizes the three principles of the Accelerated Schools philosophy:

- Students are working together with a unity of purpose to achieve the goals of the project.
- They are empowered with responsibility to collaborate and produce the video from start to finish.
- Students build on their strengths as tasks are assigned to individual members of their cooperative learning group and then they work as a team to achieve the goals of the action plan.

Video production is an effective instructional technique that captures the interest and sparks academic motivation of at-risk students because it is an active, powerful learning experience in which the students are totally involved from start to finish.

Self-Paced Instruction

At-risk students seem to like the idea of self-paced instruction. Sometimes, however, the concept "self-paced" can mean different things to the students versus the teachers. The following incident that occurred to one of us (Carrie Eidson) depicts just such a situation:

"Dr. Eidson, can I talk to you for a minute?" Jay asked me, as he sauntered into my office and plopped into the first rocking chair. Jay is a natural leader who is learning to channel his leadership abilities in positive ways. Slowly, he has developed a sense of responsibility and dropped the defiant and argumentative attitude.

"What's on your mind, Jay?" I asked, as I noticed a piece of paper in his hand.

"This is an Accelerated school, right? And the kids in this school get a say in school procedures, right?"

I nodded yes and could see the excitement mount on his face.

"The juniors and seniors have been talking about how we'd like to be treated more like junior college kids. You know, we want our courses to be self-paced. I have a petition with all the juniors' and seniors' names on it. We even wrote out how we'd like to do the self-paced with our courses."

The students' idea of self-paced is to have the teachers write the assignments, discussion topics, activities, and group projects on the board or chart paper for an entire week. This allows the students to self-pace their work around scheduled discussions and planned group activities. All work has to be completed by Friday afternoon. This also frees the teachers to work with small groups and act as facilitators for students individually on the computer or individual projects.

The staff has implemented a modification for the learning disabled students and students who have difficulty organizing their time and responsibilities. These students feel more comfortable with activities listed by the day instead of the week. The students are still free to work on the activities in any order they choose, but they know each item has to be completed on the day it is scheduled.

Self-paced instruction works very effectively with at-risk students as it gives them some control over the learning process. It teaches the students organization skills and responsibility. End-of-the-year survey results indicate the students like seeing the day or week's activity schedule visually displayed. The students indicate they feel "more grown up" when they can self-pace themselves and less pressured about deadlines.

Our staff survey indicates that staff members enjoy the self-paced instruction as it allows them to be more of facilitators, freeing them for more one-on-one small group instruction and conferences with the students. Interviews with staff members reveal that the more they became involved with the students individually and in small groups, the more the students became motivated and focused. The staff attributes this to the self-paced instruction.

But with the deepening of their involvement and bonding with the students through the self-paced component, the staff found that the majority of the at-risk students were content with receiving a D grade. This realization led to the staff using the inquiry process to develop a possible solution to the lack of motivation to higher achievement. It was decided the staff needed to model higher academic expectations for the students and make the grading system compatible with the Accelerated Schools philosophy. Hence, "A, B, C, Incomplete" became the grading system that works.

Independent Study Contract

As at-risk students experience more and more academic success and higher self-esteem at school, they become interested and motivated to stay in school and graduate. Many of the at-risk students who enter alternative schools have failed one or more grade levels and are no longer scheduled to graduate with their friends or with their original graduating class. As they become more confident in their academic abilities and rely on their strengths and talents, these students become motivated to catch up and graduate with their original class. It is at this point that many of these youth opt to take additional classes in the form of *independent study contracts.*

The independent study contract is designed and developed collaboratively between the student and the teacher in charge of a specific course of study. The student must meet all the course objectives just as if he or she were enrolled in the class during its regularly scheduled time during the regular school day. The student completes research, activities, and projects independently, meeting with the teacher a minimum of 1½ hours per week.

Depending on how motivated the student is with regard to his or her independent study course, the student can conceivably earn two to three credits beyond the usual seven to eight credits earned per year in a traditional high school.

Cultural Exchanges
Through Off-Site Experiences

One aspect of educating today's at-risk students is to help them explore and discover the world outside of their immediate community in order to expand their knowledge base. Too often, these youth only glimpse the world through the tainted pictures of television and movies. The only culture they are exposed to is the culture of their own community.

Many schools throughout America take their students on field trips as a reward or an end-of-the-year class activity. The term "field trip" usually connotes a fun, relaxing, social day. Typically, teachers do not prepare the students for where they are going or why they are going. Fun, social types of trips are worthwhile for social behavior development and peer relationship building, but the majority of trips away from school should be academically focused.

To create an atmosphere of learning through serious academic research in real-life situations should be the focus of student field trips. We use the term "off-site experiences" instead of "field trips" to relay to our students that our trips off campus are related to the information and concepts presented in their subject courses. Off-site experiences usually are one part of a thematic unit in a specific course.

Prior to an off-site experience, the teachers prepare students on why they will be visiting a specific place. The students have already been introduced to and are learning concepts and information in the thematic unit. Projects are usually built around the off-site experience or culminate with the off-site experience. Students are given a study guide or specific instructions on what to observe or participate in while on the off-site experience.

The following are some examples of off-site experiences that are part of specific thematic units:

- Research the various aspects and factors in the issue of homelessness in America. Include an off-site experience at an actual homeless shelter in which the students can talk with the residents and help out for a day.
- While studying World War II or prejudice, prepare an off-site experience to the city's history museum or Holocaust museum. Plan a project as a result of this experience.
- While studying deviant behavior, crime, the justice system, or social behavior, prepare an off-site experience to the nearest prison that will allow the students to participate in a "going straight" program taught by the inmates. Prepare activities or a study guide to reinforce this experience.
- While studying the Constitution and American court system, plan an off-site experience for the students to observe an actual criminal or civil trial. Prepare activities to conduct with the students before and after the off-site experience to reinforce the information learned.

- Research various ethnic cultures, their values, beliefs, traditions, and customs. Plan an off-site experience to an ethnic community celebration, museum, or cultural event to reinforce the students' research findings.

Off-site experiences are very valuable in helping at-risk students relate learned academic information to real-life situations. They are active learning experiences whereby the at-risk students can actively participate in the learning process. Off-site experiences challenge the students to use their critical thinking and observation skills while solving problems; analyzing the information presented; and relating the experience to their life, values, and beliefs.

Community Service Learning

Community Service Learning is an excellent instructional technique to combine academic information and social responsibility with student service projects in their community. It also provides the avenue to incorporate character education values such as the following:

- Compassion
- Honesty
- The work ethic
- Moral reasoning
- Empathy
- Perseverance
- Responsibility
- Cooperation

Typically, at-risk students do not know how to give back to their community; nor are they inclined to volunteer in any way. These young people are too caught up in their own lives, fighting for their basic needs and a place to belong, to extend themselves to others. They often have feelings of alienation and a separateness from their community. These students view their community as a place and a people that have forgotten them as the community grows and prospers. At-risk students tend to create a facade in which they do not need anyone and in which they do not want anyone to need them. Community Service Learning projects break through this facade and helps begin the bonding process of students to their community. Ray's first Community Service Learning project is a case in point:

"Dr. Eidson, can Ray speak to you please?" Mrs. Sanders, a teacher of at-risk students asked one of us on the morning of our school's first Community Service Day of the school year. "Ray is refusing to participate in the Community Service project at Miss Carter's house today. Our group is ready to walk to Miss Carter's house and Ray is holding us up."

"Go ahead with your group, Mrs. Sanders. I'll drive Ray over later," I replied as Ray grunted loudly and sat defiantly in my office. "What's the problem, Ray?"

"I don't want to go to some old lady's house and rake leaves and paint her porch. I don't work for anyone unless I get paid." he told me defiantly, looking me straight in the eyes. "I'm not going to work for nothing!"

"Sorry, opting out is not a choice at this school. You signed a commitment paper to willingly participate in the Community School's program and activities.

You were informed that Community Service Learning projects are an integral part of our curriculum," I calmly informed him. Ray looked so tough and hard sitting next to me. His jaw was clenched and he stared straight ahead when I mentioned the commitment paper he signed. "Miss Carter is 77 years old and needs our help to prepare for the winter. Her home is the only thing she has left and it's falling apart."

"So? What are my choices?"

"Either let me drive you to Miss Carter's and you actually pitch in and work or you can stay at school to clean the windows and floors. At least if you go to Miss Carter's, you can work with your friends."

"All right, let's go," Ray grudgingly said as he rose from the chair.

I saw Ray later that afternoon when the groups returned from their projects. I motioned for Ray to come talk to me in the hall.

"Well, I see you didn't die from raking leaves at Miss Carter's."

"You know, that old lady made us cookies and lemonade? She kept thanking us over and over again for helping her." Ray was smiling and shaking his head in disbelief. "She really did need our help. Miss Carter walks with a cane, you know, and there's no way she could of raked those leaves or painted that porch. Did you know Miss Carter lives all by herself and doesn't have any kids or other family to help her?"

"Yes, I knew that. I also know she's a pretty independent lady and would never consent to leave her house and live in a retirement community."

"She needed us, Dr. Eidson, and she kept thanking us and talking to us the whole time we were there." Ray was still excited. "Our group is going back to her house on the next Community Service Day."

Community Service Learning projects are most effective when developed around a thematic unit utilizing the concepts and skills from across the curriculum. The students utilize the inquiry process and develop action plans to achieve the goals of the Community Service Learning project. The students also develop and practice specific character education values that are incorporated in each unit. At-risk students appear to enjoy doing Community Service Learning projects with small groups of students rather than individually. Our own experiences indicate that at-risk students will not participate in Community Service Learning projects outside of school hours.

Research, writing, building communication skills, math, reading, English, science, social studies, art, music, home economics, and other curriculum skills are incorporated in each thematic unit. Students must research the topic being studied, such as graffiti, and develop an action plan for conducting a community graffiti awareness campaign. The action plan depicts the strategies and objectives that will be accomplished through the Community Service Learning project designed by the students and their teacher. At the end of the unit, students write a *reflection paper* on their experiences during the Community Service Learning project. The teacher and principal then write personal comments on the students' reflection papers as part of authentic assessment and acceptance of the students.

In an Accelerated alternative school, Community Service Learning projects provide the students with powerful learning experiences, unity of purpose, empowerment with responsibility, and a chance to be needed while building on their strengths. These projects provide many opportunities to incorporate character education values in the units and awaken in the students a lifelong interest in and commitment to giving back to their community. The actual projects provide at-risk students with many opportunities for problem solving, interacting socially with their peers and people in the community, raising their self-esteem, and coming to know their strengths and talents.

Chapter Summary

When the at-risk student first comes to an Accelerated alternative school, he or she has experienced many years of frustration, low motivation, low achievement, low self-esteem, and school failure. There are many factors that contribute to these young people being at risk for dropping out of school, including the following:

- Social and cultural issues and barriers
- Incompatibility of their cognitive learning style with traditional teaching and learning styles in regular schools
- Passive learning experiences
- Unnurturing school climates

By the time the at-risk student enrolls in an Accelerated alternative school, he or she usually has a history of one or more of the following:

- Truancy
- Poor attendance
- 2 to 3 years below reading level of age peers
- Aggressive or disruptive behavior
- Complete withdrawal
- Depression
- Suicidal tendencies
- Drug abuse
- Negative, sullen attitude

It is the responsibility of educators to break through these walls of failure and help each at-risk student to have faith in himself or herself to reach his or her full potential.

The establishment of the Community School and the Caring Communities Cadre has helped many students successfully stay in school in the face of difficult family situations and social barriers. We have found through our experiences in dealing with students at risk as the Community School Principal and the Superintendent of Schools in the Meramec Valley R-III School District that we need to be careful to not view these students as the problem but rather examine the outside factors that place them in at-risk situations or circumstances. The social issues, life circumstances, and educational culture are the core forces that create an environment for these students to be at risk for school failure.

To help these students develop personal academic confidence and a motivation to learn and stay in school, the Accelerated alternative school utilizes different instructional techniques from those used in the typical traditional middle and high school. Utilizing the Accelerated Schools philosophy and the Caring Communities philosophy sets the framework and focus on active participation of the students, parents, and staff in all aspects of the learning process. In the Accelerated alternative school, the focus of curriculum and instruction is on the following:

- Empowering the students with responsibility for their own learning
- Joining students together to work toward a unity of purpose in mastering skills and concepts
- Helping students learn to build on their strengths and the strengths of others through individual and group problem-solving projects
- Developing instructional techniques that encourage collaboration
- Encouraging active involvement utilizing the multiple intelligences

This chapter focuses on a few instructional techniques that have proven to be effective in capturing the interest of and motivating learning in at-risk students. Cooperative learning experiences, Whole Language, technology, Community Service, multiple intelligences, and cognitive learning field-dependent strategies provide effective powerful learning experiences for these students. These instructional techniques give the students some control in their learning process, which helps develop a sense of accomplishment and purpose in their lives.

An Accelerated alternative school demands the use of a challenging curriculum that relates learned academic information and knowledge to real-life situations. Critical thinking skills, problem-solving skills, communication skills, and social skills are fostered through a challenging curriculum based on powerful learning experiences and multiple intelligences. In real-life situations, children of all ages use their senses in exploring and discovering the world around them. Why should educational instruction be any different?

Providing challenging, powerful learning experiences through the instructional techniques described in this chapter is one aspect of creating a school where at-risk students feel a sense of belonging, control, and academic and social confidence. The other aspect needing to be considered and planned for is creating an environment that contributes to decreasing discipline problems in the school family. Academic progress stalls in schools that are riddled with discipline problems and disruptions. Most discipline codes are punitive, leaving little dignity or control over consequences with the students. The next chapter discusses various ways to create an environment that decreases disciplinary problems.

8

Reducing Discipline Problems

"If you punish a child for being naughty, and reward
him for being good, he will do right merely for the sake
of the reward; and when he goes out into the world and
finds that goodness is not always rewarded, nor wickedness
always punished, he will grow into a man who only thinks
about how he may get on in the world and does right or
wrong according as he finds advantage to himself."

Immanuel Kant
(Kohn, 1996, p. 22)

In dealing with at-risk students, the subjects of discipline and low self-esteem
seem to be entwined as major issues. These students can be very difficult to
work with in the classroom, cafeteria, hallways, and any other place in the school.
In dealing with the behaviors of at-risk youth day in and day out, teachers and
administrators can "burn out" in a short time, as we see in our field observations
and interviews.

Traditional schools generally use a variety of packaged discipline programs
such as Discipline With Dignity, Assertive Discipline, and Cooperative Discipline. These programs are based on bribes, threats, and punishments that in turn
may alienate, humiliate, anger, and inhibit long-term internal motivation for children to become lifelong learners and accept personal social responsibility. Discipline techniques from these programs force teachers and administrators to "do
things *to* students rather than working *with* students to solve problems" (Kohn,
1996, p. 73). It is a matter of teachers and administrators wanting complete control over the students. In these schools, there cannot be found a sense of community or student input into the rules or consequences.

According to John Goodlad's (1984) survey, 80% of the parents, students,
and staff in junior high schools and senior high schools across the country indicated student misbehavior and drug and alcohol use were their greatest concern
about schools. In 1996, the statistics from a community needs assessment conducted throughout Missouri by William Woods University (Bennett, 1997) indicate a rise in student discipline problems and drug and alcohol use in our state's
schools according to staff, parents, and students. We know that Missouri is not
alone in this rise in student discipline problems and drug and alcohol use in
schools, which indicates a need to find solutions to decrease these problems in
schools and communities throughout our country.

Punitive punishments that set the misbehaving student apart from his or her classmates are a staple in American educational institutions. Discipline codes are developed with a hierarchy of consequences for each offense. Consequences for misbehavior include the following:

- In-school suspension
- Out-of-school suspension
- After-school detention
- Loss of privileges (i.e., recess, free time, assemblies, trips, etc.)
- Verbal humiliation by the teacher in front of other classmates
- Moving a student's desk into the hallway or away from the other students
- Assigning extra homework
- Lowering a grade on an assignment

These punishments not only make students pay a price but also strip the students of their dignity while lowering their self-esteem. Punishment, as a tool for controlling youth, does not work in the long term because it does not teach the students appropriate behavior and social choices. It does not help students internalize right rather than wrong values; rather, punishment teaches them to avoid being caught misbehaving in the future.

Using punishment for controlling student behavior has a damaging effect on student-teacher and student-principal relationships. The at-risk student who continually receives in-school suspensions or out-of-school suspensions comes to view teachers and principals as uncaring dictators and enforcers. Rapport and trust between the student and these adults never get a chance to develop.

As the authors, we do not advocate discarding discipline codes totally. We realize that there must be a set of rules and limits in which staff, students, and parents know the parameters of expected student behavior. We agree that for the safety of all the students and staff there needs to be swift action for students bringing weapons and drugs to school. We advocate securing student, staff, and parent input and consensus in the development of school rules and discipline problems, however. This allows school pride, ownership, and responsibility to grow in all parties involved in the school.

At-risk students who enroll in an Accelerated alternative school bring with them a myriad of behaviors, beliefs, and values, most of which are socially inappropriate. For example, these students come to the Community School after experiencing years of academic failure, discipline problems, and dysfunctional peer and adult relationships. As previously stated, we find that at-risk students come from dysfunctional families in which there is little or no emotional support or nurturing. They do not see role modeling of values such as honesty, trust, responsibility, respect, compassion, cooperation, kindness, or empathy in their family or group of friends. Many belong to gangs in which they can have that much needed sense of belonging as a substitute for family.

An Accelerated alternative school builds a Caring Community and a family through the collaborative effort of the staff, students, and parents. As the feeling of "family" grows, class disruptions, fighting, and power struggles subside. Our personal experience with at-risk students is a marked decrease in the number of in-school suspensions and out-of-school suspensions as the students develop a sense of belonging and acceptance in their school community. This chapter discusses the components necessary to develop a sense of belonging, trust, security, and responsibility in all the stakeholders of the school.

Building a Caring Community is a philosophy, a belief system, in which students learn to lower their walls and allow others to really get to know them as unique worthwhile individuals. The Accelerated Schools philosophy emphasizes building a Caring Community through the utilization of the three principles of empowerment with responsibility, unity of purpose, and building on strengths. The Circle of Courage is a philosophy that allows at-risk students to develop a sense of belonging, mastery, independence, and generosity in the school environment (Brendtro et al., 1990). All three philosophies complement each other in developing a sense of community and family in the school. Each of these philosophies, when embraced and practiced by the staff, students, and parents, is effective in decreasing discipline problems with at-risk students. When meshed together, these three philosophies form a powerful tool for creating a true Caring Community and a family for the at-risk youth.

We have seen through our experiences at the Community School, visits to other alternative schools across the country, and a review of the literature that as the school environment changes into a Caring Community, academic interest and motivation increases and discipline problems decrease. An Accelerated alternative school has the responsibility of not only teaching academics but also providing experiences in a safe, accepting environment to enable at-risk students to internalize how their behavior affects others either negatively or positively and find solutions to their problems.

Impact of Self-Esteem on Discipline Problems

A review of recent literature indicates that students with high self-esteem academically achieve better and have less discipline problems than students with low self-esteem. Students' self-esteem impacts school-related areas such as the following:

- Attendance
- Class disruptions
- Violent behavior
- Completion of homework
- Participation in extracurricular actives
- Graduation rate (Canfield, 1990)

Young people's self-esteem is influenced either positively or negatively by their family's, community's, and school's nurturing and attention given to them over the course of their lives. If they are continually made to feel unworthy and inferior, students may become disruptive, negative, and defiant in order to have some control over their situation while seeking attention from peers and adults.

Packaged self-esteem-building curriculums or prosocial student workbooks "turn off" at-risk students. They see no relationship between activity pages in a workbook on such topics as Making Friends, Communication Skills, and Peer Pressure with life situations they find in their family, school, and community. Skills for building self-esteem and appropriate social behaviors are extremely important for at-risk students to assimilate and internalize. These skills have more meaning and are internalized more quickly by young people when practiced in real-life situations, however.

We advocate that teachers of at-risk students incorporate self-esteem-building strategies into everyday activities along with modeling appropriate social behaviors and treating students with respect and dignity. By following these recommendations, the staff creates an environment of acceptance, belonging, security, and trust for all students in the school.

Many teachers and principals think that setting up rewards for students raises self-esteem. Rewards are not good for producing long-term high self-esteem. At-risk students can be manipulative and "play the game," pretending to be compliantly following the rules in order to get the reward.

Rewards in and of themselves do not help students internalize values and appropriate social behavior. Rewards do not allow students to recognize their accomplishments or achievements as a personal victory; rather, they see rewards as a means to get a tangible payoff. When students can look objectively at what they have achieved through hard work and perseverance, they begin to internalize these values and know they are capable and intelligent. It is at this point that our students' personal confidence, motivation, and self-esteem begin to rise. It is at this point that students do not feel the need to seek negative attention and disruptive behaviors begin to decrease.

As their self-esteem rises, students are better able to deal with frustration and constructive criticism. Classroom observations show us that at-risk students tend to try to solve problems in appropriate ways as they begin to believe in their abilities and importance as worthwhile human beings in the school.

College students preparing to become teachers, along with practicing teachers and administrators, are continually challenged to build positive self-esteem in their students in order to decrease discipline problems. Many teachers have tried numerous activity worksheets and specific curriculums that promise to raise students' self-esteem and enable them to become problem solvers. Self-esteem activities conducted in isolation a few times per week generally do not produce the results anticipated or advertised.

Why do these strategies not work? All students, whether in at-risk situations or not, develop positive self-esteem through an environment that is caring, accepting, challenging, and nonthreatening. Isolated activities have no relevance to at-risk students' lives and immediate situations. Raising students' self-esteem is a process in which we help the students positively interact with their family, school, and community.

The story of Jamie, a young man one of us (Carrie Eidson) observed at the Community School, shows these forces in action.

Outside the Circle

Jamie, his mother, two little sisters, one older brother, and his mother's boyfriend live in a four-room shack at the edge of town among the poorest of the poor. Jamie's mother and her boyfriend snort cocaine and drink alcohol. Neither adult works but both seem to always have money. Jamie is truly a gifted young man and should attend college. He came to the Community School in the fall because he was constantly truant and failing courses at the traditional high school. His attitude was sullen and extremely negative when he first arrived at our school.

One Monday morning in November, Jamie burst into my office and immediately started rocking violently in the rocking chair across from my desk. I joined him, sitting in the other rocking chair, leaving my desk for a more nonthreatening turf. Jamie was a mess! His long hair was disheveled, his rock band shirt was wrinkled, and he looked like he had been awake all night. I waited for him to speak, giving him time to collect his thoughts and harness his emotions.

"I'm probably going to get in trouble today, but I came to school anyway. There's no food in the house and I figured I could get breakfast and lunch here." Jamie stared defiantly at the wall as he made this statement. "Mom and her boyfriend got busted last night. The cops kicked in our door and made me, my sisters, my brother, and our two friends lay face down on the floor while they handcuffed my mom and her boyfriend. Then they searched every inch of our house and found lots of drugs. The cops took them both to jail. We don't have a phone, so I don't know how my mom is."

"Pretty scary situation to be in. You must have been very upset seeing your mom handcuffed. Are you all right?" I spoke softly and calmly to Jamie. "You must be worried about how she's doing in jail. Jamie, you look like you've been awake all night."

"I'm all right, just tired. I didn't have any place else to go and I didn't want to stay home alone all day." Jamie shrugged as he stared off into space. "You know, I'm getting sick and tired of my family being like this. It's the same thing all the time . . . drinking and drugging."

"But mostly, I'm afraid 'cos I know I'll end up just like them. I can see myself with three kids living in a beat-up trailer with a dead-end job. My life stinks!"

"Why do you think your only option is to follow in your mom's footsteps?" I asked him. "Don't you think you have any other options ahead of you besides living in a beat-up trailer with a dead-end job? Jamie, you are intelligent and have the ability to accomplish any goal you set for yourself. What about college? With your abilities and circumstances, you could qualify for several college scholarships. That could be one way out of this situation."

"I have dreams of being a vet, because I love working with animals. But that's all they are . . . dreams." He sighed as he spoke, still making no eye contact with me. "I don't see any way out of where I am. College? I couldn't stand being at the regular high school, how would I make it at college? Who would take care of my mom and little sisters? My big brother is a joke; he can't even take care of himself. I feel like I'm treading water and getting nowhere. It's like I don't fit in anywhere except this school."

"Why do you feel that you fit in this school?" I asked, surprised.

"Because, Dr. Eidson, you have a whole school of kids outside the circle like me." Jamie said exasperatedly. "None of us made it at the schools we came from. Teachers there always thought we were stupid 'cos we didn't do homework or brownnose in class. Most of us never went to school that much 'cos nobody cared if we did or not. The truth is that those schools were boring and I knew half the stuff they taught anyway!

"The teachers never really cared about kids like me. All we'd ever do is read stuff on our own, answer questions, and take notes from the teacher doing all the talking. I learned more from the talk shows on TV. I never felt like anything I was supposed to learn at that other high school was going to make a big difference in my life. At least here, the teachers notice me and talk to me about stuff that's important to me. They even ask my opinion on stuff!"

"Actually, you are learning the same material as you did at your other school, only in a different way," I explained.

"Yeah, but it's different here. We do more talking in class about our ideas and we can make projects about stuff we learn instead of doing boring reports all of the time."

Jamie looked at me for the first time since he had come into my office.

"I guess the most important thing is you guys at this school don't think we're losers. I think you guys understand where we're coming from . . . can I borrow your phone to call the police station and see if I can talk to my mom?"

Student-Teacher Relationships—The Key

Our nation's schools are full of students like Jamie who feel "outside the circle." Nothing decreases behavior problems as much as the student-teacher relationship. Teachers build trusting relationships with their students by taking the time to listen to them and really hearing their words as well as the feelings that are not spoken. The teachers of at-risk youth work to create a climate of family not only in individual classrooms but in the cafeteria, the hallways, and the parking lot through showing genuine warmth and concern for all students in the school community. These teachers take the time to talk *with* and laugh *with* their students, which builds the bonds of trust and security. At-risk students can smell a phony a mile away, so teachers must look for character traits they can genuinely like about each student and build their relationship from there. Usually, every student bonds with at least one teacher, secretary, the principal, or paraprofessional through this procedure. Discipline problems decrease as the student-staff relationship grows strong and firm.

Through interviewing and observing at-risk students and master teachers of at-risk students, we see that as their relationship grows deeper, the students are more apt to share their feelings and accept responsibility for their inappropriate behavior. At this point in the relationship, teachers can discuss openly with the students other choices they can make and how their positive or negative behavior affects others. The teachers' responsibility is to help their students internalize appropriate behavior and a sound value system. The following interview shows the positive impact strong student-teacher relationships have on discipline problems:

> One of us (Carrie Eidson) asked three seniors who had been at the Community School for 3 years to come talk to me about their views on how to decrease student discipline problems. As I looked at them sitting in my office, I remembered back to when each of these young people came to this school. The staff and I were privileged to see a marvelous transformation in Adam, Molly, and Jay during our time with them. Their rough edges were all but gone, along with the tough, sullen attitudes and defiant behavior. I saw before me three soon-to-be graduates possessing a new, strong, positive self-confidence and maturity.
>
> "I asked you to come talk with me about how we can decrease discipline problems without using in-school suspension or out-of-school suspension," I began. "We have all seen such a major change in the three of you since you came here 3 years ago. What brought about the change? Was it just the natural maturing that comes with age?"
>
> Jay was the first to speak. "Well, part of it is just growing up a little, I guess. But mainly, we've gotten to know the teachers here as real people and they know us as real people. You don't want to act like a dork or idiot in front of people you like and respect!"
>
> "Yeah, like I can trust most of the teachers if I want to tell them about things I've done in the past and not feel stupid," Adam chimed in as he learned forward in the rocking chair with an intense look on his face. Wild and severely defiant Adam had changed the most over the years, learning to control his temper and talk out his anger. "I can feel free to come in your office and tell you how angry I am with my mom or anyone because you listen and you know me really well. The other thing is you guys show you really care, like the way you will come pick us up if we miss the bus or our cars won't start so we don't miss school. I mean, you guys really mean it when you tell us the only thing you won't tolerate is us not coming to school. No other teacher or principal in the other schools would drive all the way out to my house if I called and said my truck won't start."

"For me, I guess I realized that you guys weren't going to kick me out when I was angry and acting like a jerk. I don't know when it was, but somewhere along the way, I felt like I belonged here. And like Jay said, you don't want to act like a pout-face brat in front of adults you care about," Molly quietly told our little group. Molly is the deep thinker and our independent spirit who came to us filled with hurt and rage for all adults. Because of her extremely high intelligence and the thick walls she built around herself, it took a long time for Molly to develop a bond of trust with any staff member.

"Building these relationships took time. Do you think there is any way to speed up the process for new students as they join our school?" I was fascinated by these students' insights and reflections.

"Dr. Eidson, you gotta understand where the new kids are coming from when they first come to this school." Jay gently lectures me as if I was the student and he was the principal. "The new kids have always been in trouble at their old schools so they don't respect any teachers or principals. They come in your office and see you as the enemy because they're used to getting punished by the principal. Sorry, it must be the nature of your job—kind of goes with the territory." Jay laughed at this, then proceeded. "They don't know that they can trust you and the staff . . . that this school is different."

"Doing that low ropes course and team-building stuff at the beginning of each school year helps get the teachers and students close," Molly ventured. "We like how it was done at a camp instead of at the school. We had no choice but to work with our team members to finish the ropes course."

"Yeah, that was fun and I got to know kids I wouldn't have normally picked as friends," Adam added.

The four of us decided it might be a good idea to share this conversation with the staff and other students to see if they might have any other ideas to speed up the relationship process. The staff agreed that the keys to decreasing discipline problems are to build genuine relationships of caring and concern with the students and build an environment of family and community in the school. We then showed this information to the student body, staff, and parents. The Discipline Cadre decided to survey the students on this issue. The results indicated 90% of the students felt the student-teacher relationship and school environment are the keys to decreasing discipline problems.

Teachers of at-risk students have an enormous impact on their students' expectations for personal accomplishments and self-esteem. Teachers who suggest to their students that they are highly capable and intelligent enough to tackle challenging tasks can raise students' perception of their academic abilities. We are constantly telling our students how capable and intelligent they are and that we will not accept work that does not reflect their true abilities. After hearing this over and over, our students start behaving and producing better.

How do we build strong bonds and relationships with at-risk youth?

Utilizing the Circle of Courage, Accelerated Schools, and Caring Communities Philosophy to Decrease Discipline Problems

The foundation of a responsible, motivated, curious, academically confident, and intelligent child is an environment of caring, acceptance, nurturing, and respect. Children's self-esteem and self-respect are based on the following:

- Their perception of their importance to peers and adults
- Their perception of their worthiness as a person
- Their perception of the amount of personal control they have over their life and environment
- Their perceptions of their academic and social competence
- Their perceptions of their strength and talent areas
- Their perception of their place in their family
- Their perception of their future life circumstances

The at-risk students who find their way to an alternative school tend to have distorted perceptions of themselves and display inappropriate behavioral responses to peers, adults, and life situations. According to Brendtro et al. (1990), these students display a variety of behaviors such as bullying, cheating, distrustfulness, delinquency, selfishness, lack of respect, irresponsibility, and manipulativeness. They also give up easily, avoid risks or take too many risks, and play martyr or poor victim. Their self-esteem, self-respect, and trust levels are very low.

When at-risk students are invited into a Caring Community, their self-esteem, self-respect, and trust levels start to rise. As these rise, motivation for learning and behaving well also rise. Brendtro et al. (1990) discuss creating a caring or reclaiming environment for at-risk students. They advocate using the Native American "Circle of Courage" philosophy, whereby the school community creates an environment of belonging, mastery, independence, and generosity. The goal is to establish or promote productive, literate, and caring young people who can contribute positively to the community in which they live.

The Circle of Courage philosophy complements and meshes quite easily with the Accelerated Schools philosophy, the Caring Communities philosophy and the recommendations in the NASSP and Carnegie Foundation (1996) report *Breaking Ranks: Changing an American Institution*. By utilizing all of these philosophies in the alternative school program, the students, staff, parents, and community members create a caring environment and community. All of these philosophies are steeped in sound educational and psychological practices and theories that foster security, acceptance, trust, motivation, independence, and responsibility in at-risk students.

The following pages describe the necessary components for building a Caring Community utilizing the Circle of Courage and Accelerated Schools philosophies to speed up the process of relationship building while decreasing discipline problems and raising students' self-esteem in the school environment. Sample forms for helping to create an environment to decrease discipline problems can be found in the Resources section.

Building a bridge of trust and belonging is the first major step in developing a strong relationship with at-risk students while decreasing discipline problems. Reaching out to let these young people know and understand that the staff accepts them as they are and is genuinely concerned about their needs can be accomplished through the following:

- Utilizing an accepting and warm tone of voice and facial expressions when talking with students.
- Always talking *with* students, not *to* them. Talk with students as you would a friend or co-worker. In an Accelerated alternative school, the students and staff are co-workers in every sense of the word.

- Being genuine and welcoming each student each day into the school or the classroom.
- Taking an interest in students' lives outside of school by really listening to what they describe, fear, dream, anguish over, and enjoy.
- Constantly drawing all students into discussions. Ask their opinions on big matters and small matters. Use their input in decisions to be made.
- Developing a strong rapport with the parents of the students in school. This positively impacts the teacher's rapport and relationship with the students.
- Hugging or laying hands on student's shoulders to let them know you care about and are interested in them.
- If a student is having a bad day or wrestling with a problem or crisis, placing a phone call that night to the student at home to make sure he or she is all right.

Create "Family Groups" of seven to nine students and one adult. Schedule Family Time 15 to 20 minutes each day in place of advisory or home room. The Family Leader (the adult) is responsible for monitoring the academic and behavioral progress of each student in his/her family. Every 2 weeks, the Family Leader makes a phone call or sends a postcard to each student's parents informing them of the academic and behavioral progress of their child.

Family Time is for bonding with the students and discovering their talents, feelings, ideas, problems, and interests. It is a time to discuss and give input into school procedures, events, off-site experiences, or anything the students want to explore. Individual goal setting for such things as attendance, attitude, work habits, and behavior also takes place during Family Time. Adult Family Leaders are teachers, classroom aides, secretaries, and counselors.

Empowering students with responsibility and control over their learning and behavior is the second major step in developing a strong student-teacher relationship. Encouraging independence and appropriate risk taking gives at-risk students back their dignity and control while raising their self-esteem and teaching responsibility.

- Empowering at-risk students with responsibility cannot happen overnight. Remember, these youth are used to years of tight control, rigid rules, and few opportunities for personal choice in their experiences at the traditional school. At first, at-risk students want the empowerment but not the responsibility. Responsibility has to be taught slowly with a great deal of patience and perseverance.
- Give students positions of responsibility around the school.
- Allow students to plan assemblies and off-site experiences with the staff.
- Allow and encourage students to give input and plan school procedures, rules, and goals through being on school cadres.

Each staff member and his or her class write the rules for the classroom. Students are not given written Misconducts unless the infraction is deemed serious enough for the student to be sent to the principal immediately. Staff members handle behavior problems in their classrooms through the following:

- Practicing patience
- Resisting getting into power struggles with the students
- Letting a student calm down first, then talking with the student about appropriate behavior choices
- Using natural consequences for inappropriate behavior

Student governance is very effective for implementing the school's Discipline Code, which the parents, students, and staff developed through the Discipline Cadre. The Student Governance Cadre consists of a representative from each school Family Group and one staff member. The Family Group representatives are changed every three weeks so all students in the school can serve on the Student Governance Cadre at least one time during the school year. Students who break the rules go before the Student Governance Cadre to explain why they broke the rules and how their behavior affects the other students and staff. The student's parents are notified of the meeting and asked to attend with their child.

At the daily staff meeting, individual staff members may make written student referrals to the Student Governance Cadre for help with consistent classroom behavior problems such as defiant attitude toward staff, consistently off-task, coming unprepared to class, disruptive classroom behavior, and any other problems affecting the climate and instruction of the classroom. The staff discusses the referrals and decides whether it is a problem with other teachers and staff members or just between the referring staff member and the student. If the presenting problem is affecting two or more staff members, the student is referred to the Student Governance Cadre. If it is deemed a problem between the referring staff member only and the student, this case is referred to the counselor for conflict mediation between the staff member and student.

Student Governance Cadre members discuss the inappropriate behavior with the offender and his or her parents and try to help the student decide on more appropriate behavior choices for the future. The Student Governance Cadre, the parents, and the offender write an action plan for the student to implement for the next 2 weeks. The offender must return to the Student Governance Cadre at the end of the 2-week period to report on the success or failure of meeting the goal of the action plan. The student must keep a daily log and write reflections on how he or she thinks the day went with regard to the action plan strategies and goal.

If the student did not meet the goals of his or her action plan, the Student Governance Cadre and the student decide on action plan changes to include checks and balances on the student's freedom and behavior monitoring. The student must then meet weekly with the Student Governance Cadre until appropriate behaviors show consistent improvement. If the student still does not meet his or her action plan goals after 6 to 8 weeks of interventions, the student and his or her parents must go to Home Court Review with the staff and principal.

Home Court Review is a serious conference between the student, staff, principal, and the student's parents concerning the conditions that must be met for the student to remain at the Accelerated alternative school. The student is put on official probation and the conditions that must be met are written and agreed on by all parties. (A sample form is in the Resources section.) The parents are required to call their child's Family Leader each Friday morning before school starts to check on his or her behavior progress for the week. Requiring the parents to make the call helps to ensure their involvement and commitment to their child and the school. It is another way to foster empowerment with responsibility in the parents.

Not all the students who reach the Home Court Review stage will be able to meet the conditions for remaining at the Accelerated alternative school. The reasons for this are numerous and beyond the abilities of the staff to change.

Readers should not be discouraged if a student has to be dismissed from a school. Not every at-risk student can be helped. Sometimes, there has been such deep emotional turmoil in the student and the family that their needs cannot be met in a school setting. At this point, the child is not just dismissed without a plan for getting the needed help, however. The child and his or her family are referred to the Caring Communities Cadre to receive wraparound services to help break the cycle of dysfunction in the family. The student may reapply to the school for readmission after participating in these services and making substantial and consist behavioral progress.

The principal immediately handles all serious behavior problems in which the safety of the students and the staff is at stake, such as possession or selling of drugs or weapons, assault on a staff member or another student, leaving the school grounds without permission, and anything else deemed serious by the principal and staff. These offenses do not go before the Student Governance Cadre.

Fostering independence and mastery through challenging curriculum, powerful learning experiences, and opportunities for risk taking and control build positive self-esteem and perceptions of high academic and behavioral competence in students at-risk for school failure. According to Brendtro et al. (1990), students who achieve mastery and competence over their environment, gain strong feelings of pleasure,which increases their motivation to display appropriate behavior. In most traditional American schools, the unwritten rule is that teachers must make their students comply with school rules and obey authority unquestioningly, keep tight control over how and what the students learn, and punish students who do not show absolute obedience. In this type of school or classroom, the students have no personal motivation or commitment to behave appropriately and responsibly. There is no personal incentive for the students to try to gain mastery and competence over their environment.

The following are strategies to help students develop independence and mastery over their environment:

- Receive input from the students, set realistic limits for student behavior, and be consistent.
- Communicate high academic and behavioral expectations to students and maintain the expectations until they become a reality.
- Refrain from dominating and controlling what the students must do and how they must do it to show mastery.
- Teach students how to set personal goals and develop action plans to achieve their goals.
- Be actively involved in the learning process while showing genuine interest and enjoyment in being with the students.
- Discuss "failure" with the students and what can be learned from our failures. Through acceptance and concerned gestures, facial expressions, and tone of voice, teachers can make an environment where it is OK to fail and try again. At-risk students will go to great lengths to escape the shame of failure, such as skipping school, withdrawing from the activity, indulging in disruptive behavior, feigning illness, or becoming defiant to teachers and peers.
- Give students many opportunities to make decisions, give input, and act responsibly. If at-risk students are not given some autonomy, they respond to authority with resistance or withdrawal. Self-discipline develops in teenagers if they are given opportunities to exert influence over their own lives. (Brendtro et al., 1990)

Unity of purpose and generosity must be developed in at-risk students for them to build inner connections and bonds with their peers, parents, school staff, and community. We mentioned earlier that students who have experienced continual failure, behavior problems, and dysfunctional family life do not know how to give of themselves or work cooperatively with others in real-life situations. Building on individual strengths while all students or small groups of students unite to work for a purpose allows them some control to problem-solve and make decisions to achieve their goal.

The unity of purpose principle encourages collaboration and cooperation among students and staff. Conflicts are worked out so power struggles decrease while students are taught appropriate and responsible social behavior. By creating a unity of purpose for at-risk students, an Accelerated school enables them to learn the virtue of generosity, a giving of oneself to others.

These youth have been brought up in a society where success is measured by the amount of material possessions a person owns. We live in a "me" society in which everyone looks out for "number one." Today's young people work for money to buy designer jeans, shoes, cars, and other prized possessions. They do not know how or want to help or be responsible for the welfare of others in their community. The reason these students do not want to give of themselves to others in need is that they do not want to get too close to anyone. Letting someone get close will pierce their inner wall that hides feelings and trust.

Our experiences indicate that at-risk students benefit greatly from being in-volved with Community Service projects. As these students share unselfishly of their talents, time, and efforts in these projects, their sense of self-worth increases along with their sense of belonging to the community. As these same young people give back to their community and receive praise and affirmations from others they have helped, school and community vandalism, juvenile delinquency, and violent gang activities decrease.

Collaboration Versus Competition

At-risk students do not fare well in a competitive environment. Unfortunately, traditional American schools encourage competition through such activities and events as honor roll, student of the month, grade point averages, and other re-wards for good behavior and academic achievement. Students who are at-risk for school failure generally read below grade level, have gaps in basic skills, become frustrated quite easily, and tend to give up trying to learn new information early in their school career for fear of being humiliated in front of their peers. These same students are more likely to skip school; do no homework; disrupt the class; display loud, aggressive behavior; get into power struggles with teachers; and spend many hours in the principal's office, all because they realize they cannot win in a competitive environment. The inappropriate behavior they display en-ables these students to save face in front of their peers.

In a collaborative environment, the risk of failure and humiliation is dimin-ished. Risk taking while exploring the world of knowledge is encouraged by the staff. Students work together to solve problems and help each other in the learn-ing process. Public rewards are given to all students, not just the same few. As the at-risk students collaborate on projects, learning new materials, testing possible solutions, and solving problems, motivation for learning increases while disruptive behavior decreases in the classroom and elsewhere in the school. In the collaborative environment, students and staff form bonds of trust and genuine relationships, thereby increasing a sense of belonging in the students.

Creating a collaborative, accepting, family environment in the Accelerated alternative school is a must to persuade at-risk students to feel comfortable enough to take risks and become motivated to learn. In this type of environment without competition, at-risk students find their basic emotional needs are met and discipline problems decrease. Examples of how to eliminate competition are as follows :

- Provide opportunities for all students to be recognized for individual effort, accomplishment, and improvement. (Buck-Collopy & Green, 1995)
- Require staff and students recognize others for doing "Random Acts of Kindness" each day. A Random Act of Kindness may be thanking someone for taking the time to talk with another in need or opening a door for someone. These are announced over the school intercom by the individual who received the Random Act of Kindness.
- Write to students privately, recognizing them for something they learned or a problem they solved.
- Create an awards ceremony in which each student is recognized for an accomplishment or taking on a new challenge.

Chapter Summary

Decreasing discipline problems can be achieved through creating a Caring Community and environment for the students, staff, and parents of the school. Students who are at risk for school failure do not have a sense of belonging or control over their environment. Their value systems are not intact and usually they have not had the appropriate role modeling or nurturing needed to internalize appropriate and responsible social behavior. These youth come to an alternative school distrustful of adults, either aggressive or withdrawn, and with very low levels of self-worth from years of school failure and family dysfunction.

Studies, observations, and interviews we completed indicate that the most important factor in decreasing discipline problems is building deep, genuine student-teacher relationships. Students who are in at-risk situations need and want to form strong relationships with significant adults and their peers, but fear of abandonment prohibits this from occurring outside of an accepting, nonthreatening environment. Dedicated teachers of at-risk youth build trust and bonds with their students through being genuine, accepting, warm, and honest. These teachers do not feel the need to control their students or demand unquestioning, blind obedience. They know that tangible rewards and punishments do not produce long-term changes in behavior problems.

Discipline problems decrease when the learning environment is collaborative, not competitive. At-risk students do not like to take risks or compete for fear of more failure in their lives. Competition bashes self-esteem in students who have gaps in their educational skills and social abilities. At-risk students generally perceive their academic and social competence to be low, so they resist or withdraw from competition to preserve what little self-esteem they have left.

By utilizing the Circle of Courage, Accelerated Schools philosophy, and the Caring Communities philosophy in combination, we can create an environment in which students, staff, and parents are valued, share in decision making, and are not afraid to fail while exploring the world around them. Through genuine relationships, empowerment with responsibility, building on strengths, generosity, and mastery, these young people develop a sense of belonging and independence. As at-risk students internalize how their behavior affects others and learn to deal with conflicts, power struggles, anger, and frustration, they begin to enjoy higher self-esteem and an intact value system. When this begins to happen, discipline problems decrease while motivation and interest in learning increase.

Creating a Caring Community and accepting environment does decrease discipline problems. As one student so eloquently summarized why his grades improved and his behavior problems ceased,

> When the teachers really care about you as a person and really know everything about you . . . they are your friends. And nobody wants to act stupid or ignorant to friends. Somewhere along the line, you realize this school is a family that you are a part of and you don't want to hurt your family. You know what I mean? It's like the anger just sort of leaves when you know you belong and that they really want you here.

Resources

The following pages contain sample forms for the reader to use as guides. We urge the reader to create forms that are specific to the needs of the at-risk students and school districts that will be involved in becoming an Accelerated alternative school.

PARENT TAKING STOCK AND VISION SURVEY

Please help us determine appropriate and effective programs for our district school children by completing this survey. We are trying to address the problem of students dropping out of school before graduating with a high school diploma. Please place a check mark (✓) by the answer that best describes your feelings and opinions in response to the questions.

Thank you for your help and input in this matter.

The School District Administration

1. Having my child graduate from high school is a priority to me.
   ( ) Strongly Agree
   ( ) Agree
   ( ) Neutral
   ( ) Disagree
   ( ) Strongly Disagree

2. Parents have a strong influence on their children in today's society.
   ( ) Strongly Agree
   ( ) Agree
   ( ) Neutral
   ( ) Disagree
   ( ) Strongly Disagree

3. I expect and want my child to _____ after graduating from high school.
   ( ) Go to work full-time
   ( ) Attend a junior college
   ( ) Attend a vocational technical school
   ( ) Attend a 4-year college
   ( ) Join the military

4. As a parent, I want to be involved with my child's education but sometimes I do not know how.
   ( ) Strongly Agree
   ( ) Agree
   ( ) Neutral
   ( ) Disagree
   ( ) Strongly Disagree

5. I feel ill equipped sometimes to deal with the issues and problems of teenagers today.
   ( ) Strongly Agree
   ( ) Agree
   ( ) Neutral
   ( ) Disagree
   ( ) Strongly Disagree

6. Teenagers seem to get bored easily in schools today.
   ( ) Strongly Agree
   ( ) Agree
   ( ) Neutral
   ( ) Disagree
   ( ) Strongly Disagree

7. Schools should teach to each child's learning style to promote motivation and interest.

( ) Strongly Agree
( ) Agree
( ) Neutral
( ) Disagree
( ) Strongly Disagree

8. A positive, warm, accepting school climate is important to make students feel they belong.

( ) Strongly Agree
( ) Agree
( ) Neutral
( ) Disagree
( ) Strongly Disagree

9. Parents should have opportunities to provide input on all aspects of the school.

( ) Strongly Agree
( ) Agree
( ) Neutral
( ) Disagree
( ) Strongly Disagree

10. Schools need to make parents feel welcomed and at home there.

( ) Strongly Agree
( ) Agree
( ) Neutral
( ) Disagree
( ) Strongly Disagree

11. Parents should be held responsible and accountable for getting their child to attend school each day.

( ) Strongly Agree
( ) Agree
( ) Neutral
( ) Disagree
( ) Strongly Disagree

12. A close student-teacher-parent relationship helps form strong bonds of trust and motivation for the students.

( ) Strongly Agree
( ) Agree
( ) Neutral
( ) Disagree
( ) Strongly Disagree

13. I would like my child to attend a small school in order to get more teacher attention and be well known by students and staff.

( ) Strongly Agree
( ) Agree
( ) Neutral
( ) Disagree
( ) Strongly Disagree

14. I want my child to have a variety of choices and experiences that relate the information he or she learns at school to real-life situations.
    ( ) Strongly Agree
    ( ) Agree
    ( ) Neutral
    ( ) Disagree
    ( ) Strongly Disagree

15. Community Service should be included in the middle school and high school curricula.
    ( ) Strongly Agree
    ( ) Agree
    ( ) Neutral
    ( ) Disagree
    ( ) Strongly Disagree

16. My child might achieve better at a small alternative school that allows the students more choices and input into their own learning process.
    ( ) Strongly Agree
    ( ) Agree
    ( ) Neutral
    ( ) Disagree
    ( ) Strongly Disagree

17. Schools should be "family-oriented" and have a "family-style atmosphere."
    ( ) Strongly Agree
    ( ) Agree
    ( ) Neutral
    ( ) Disagree
    ( ) Strongly Disagree

18. What are some of the reasons your child has not been successful at the traditional school?
    1. _____
    2. _____
    3. _____
    4. _____

19. Name three (3) things you would like to see implemented at your child's school to make it more of a family school.
    1. _____
    2. _____
    3. _____

20. I would like communication between my child's teachers and me every 2 weeks with regard to his or her academic and behavioral progress.
    ( ) Strongly Agree
    ( ) Agree
    ( ) Neutral
    ( ) Disagree
    ( ) Strongly Disagree

21. I would be actively involved in school decision making if I knew my input was really wanted and needed.
    ( ) Strongly Agree
    ( ) Agree
    ( ) Neutral
    ( ) Disagree
    ( ) Strongly Disagree

22. I would participate in night meetings more if baby-sitting was provided for my younger children.
    ( ) Yes
    ( ) No

23. I would participate in night meetings more if transportation could be arranged.
    ( ) Yes
    ( ) No

24. I would support and participate in Parent-Student-Staff Community Service Days.
    ( ) Yes
    ( ) No

25. I would support and participate in Parent-Student-Staff School Planning sessions if I was personally called to participate.
    ( ) Yes
    ( ) No

STUDENT TAKING STOCK AND VISION SURVEY

This survey is to be given to all Middle School and High School students to find out their ideas and feelings toward school. Please place a check mark (✓) by the answer that best describes your answer to the question. Please fill in answers to questions requiring a written response.

Thank you for your help in this matter.

The Staff

1. I feel comfortable and accepted by the other students and staff at my regular Middle School or High School.
   ( ) Strongly Agree
   ( ) Agree
   ( ) Neutral
   ( ) Disagree
   ( ) Strongly Disagree

2. I feel close to my teachers.
   ( ) Strongly Agree
   ( ) Agree
   ( ) Neutral
   ( ) Disagree
   ( ) Strongly Disagree

3. I am involved in extracurricular clubs and activities at the regular Middle School or High School.
   ( ) Yes
   ( ) No

4. I have to work after school, so I cannot participate in after school activities.
   ( ) Yes
   ( ) No

5. I can talk to my teachers about anything that is important to me.
   ( ) Yes
   ( ) No

6. I feel a close student-teacher relationship is very important.
   ( ) Strongly Agree
   ( ) Agree
   ( ) Neutral
   ( ) Disagree
   ( ) Strongly Disagree

7. I learn best by (Please check *all* the ways you learn well):
   ( ) Lecture style
   ( ) Hands-on projects
   ( ) Class discussions
   ( ) Reading newspapers, novels, magazines
   ( ) Small group projects
   ( ) Field trips

( ) One-on-one teacher instruction
( ) Seeing displays or visual demonstrations
( ) Individual projects
( ) Reading and answering questions from a textbook
( ) Worksheets
( ) Work/study classes
( ) Using computers, videos, laser disks, videotaping
( ) Making things
( ) Listening to directions and information needed

8. Getting a high school diploma is important to me.
   ( ) Strongly Agree
   ( ) Agree
   ( ) Neutral
   ( ) Disagree
   ( ) Strongly Disagree

9. In a Middle School or High School with over 1,000 students, I would feel lost in the crowd or alienated.
   ( ) Strongly Agree
   ( ) Agree
   ( ) Neutral
   ( ) Disagree
   ( ) Strongly Disagree

10. I would like to have some control and choices in what I learn.
    ( ) Strongly Agree
    ( ) Agree
    ( ) Neutral
    ( ) Disagree
    ( ) Strongly Disagree

11. I feel there is a lot of student freedom in my traditional Middle School or High School.
    ( ) Strongly Agree
    ( ) Agree
    ( ) Neutral
    ( ) Disagree
    ( ) Strongly Disagree

12. Name three (3) characteristics you want your teachers to have:

    1. _____

    2. _____

    3. _____

13. I am motivated to attend school each day.
    ( ) Strongly Agree
    ( ) Agree
    ( ) Neutral
    ( ) Disagree
    ( ) Strongly Disagree

14. I generally miss _____ days of school per semester.

    ( ) 1-2 days
    ( ) 3-5 days
    ( ) 6-10 days
    ( ) more than 10 days

15. I would be more motivated to attend school at a smaller, alternative school.

    ( ) Yes
    ( ) No

16. I feel homework is important and worthwhile.

    ( ) Strongly Agree
    ( ) Agree
    ( ) Neutral
    ( ) Disagree
    ( ) Strongly Disagree

17. I complete my homework

    ( ) 100% of the time
    ( ) 40%-69% of the time
    ( ) 70%-99% of the time
    ( ) Below 40% of the time

18. I would like attend a school with a relaxed, family atmosphere.

    ( ) Strongly Agree
    ( ) Agree
    ( ) Neutral
    ( ) Disagree
    ( ) Strongly Disagree

19. I like a colorful "homey" classroom with bulletin boards and student work displayed.

    ( ) Strongly Agree
    ( ) Agree
    ( ) Neutral
    ( ) Disagree
    ( ) Strongly Disagree

20. I would like a classroom with couches, comfortable chairs, and tables instead of desks in a row.

    ( ) Strongly Agree
    ( ) Agree
    ( ) Neutral
    ( ) Disagree
    ( ) Strongly Disagree

21. I like awards and awards assemblies.

    ( ) Strongly Agree
    ( ) Agree
    ( ) Neutral
    ( ) Disagree
    ( ) Strongly Disagree

22. I like field trips as part of a class project.

    ( ) Strongly Agree
    ( ) Agree
    ( ) Neutral
    ( ) Disagree
    ( ) Strongly Disagree

23. I would like to attend school in the morning and work for credits in the afternoon.

    ( ) Strongly Agree
    ( ) Agree
    ( ) Neutral
    ( ) Disagree
    ( ) Strongly Disagree

24. I would like to attend school from 7:30 a.m. until 4:30 p.m. Monday through Thursday and be off school on Friday.

    ( ) Strongly Agree
    ( ) Agree
    ( ) Neutral
    ( ) Disagree
    ( ) Strongly Disagree

25. I would like to attend school on a year-round schedule in which we would attend school 9 weeks, then have 2 weeks off, for four cycles and have 6 weeks off in the summer off and 2 other weeks of vacation.

    ( ) Strongly Agree
    ( ) Agree
    ( ) Neutral
    ( ) Disagree
    ( ) Strongly Disagree

26. I would like to attend school the hours we presently attend.

    ( ) Strongly Agree
    ( ) Agree
    ( ) Neutral
    ( ) Disagree
    ( ) Strongly Disagree

COMMUNITY TAKING STOCK AND VISION SURVEY

Our school district has set a goal to prevent students from dropping out of high school before graduating and helping those that have dropped out return to school to earn their diploma. We need your input in determining the needs of the community with regard to programs and services for these students and their families. Please place a check mark (✓) by the answer that best describes your answer to the question.

Thank you for your help and support in this matter.

The School District Administration

1. Our community is a safe and healthy place for families and children to live and work.
   ( ) Strongly Agree
   ( ) Agree
   ( ) Neutral
   ( ) Disagree
   ( ) Strongly Disagree

2. Our community has enough rental homes and apartments for low-income families.
   ( ) Strongly Agree
   ( ) Agree
   ( ) Neutral
   ( ) Disagree
   ( ) Strongly Disagree

3. Landlords and homeowners need to clean up and fix up their property to help maintain property values and look pleasing to the community.
   ( ) Strongly Agree
   ( ) Agree
   ( ) Neutral
   ( ) Disagree
   ( ) Strongly Disagree

4. This community cares about families and children in need and provides enough help to them with clothing, food, shelter, etc.
   ( ) Strongly Agree
   ( ) Agree
   ( ) Neutral
   ( ) Disagree
   ( ) Strongly Disagree

5. Our community has many recreational facilities and activities for children and families.
   ( ) Strongly Agree
   ( ) Agree
   ( ) Neutral
   ( ) Disagree
   ( ) Strongly Disagree

6. Our community has a variety of leisure-time activities for children ages 13-18.
   ( ) Strongly Agree
   ( ) Agree
   ( ) Neutral

( ) Disagree

( ) Strongly Disagree

7. Our community needs a recreation center or some other places for teenagers to have safe, alcohol-free activities with their friends.

( ) Strongly Agree

( ) Agree

( ) Neutral

( ) Disagree

( ) Strongly Disagree

8. In today's society, a community that prospers economically and socially has a majority population with a high school diploma or more education.

( ) Strongly Agree

( ) Agree

( ) Neutral

( ) Disagree

( ) Strongly Disagree

9. A poorly educated community will not attract high-skill industry, small businesses, or new families to relocate there.

( ) Strongly Agree

( ) Agree

( ) Neutral

( ) Disagree

( ) Strongly Disagree

10. Teenagers who drop out of school become a financial burden to their community.

( ) Strongly Agree

( ) Agree

( ) Neutral

( ) Disagree

( ) Strongly Disagree

11. Education should be a priority for children and adults in order for them to become productive and responsible citizens in the community.

( ) Strongly Agree

( ) Agree

( ) Neutral

( ) Disagree

( ) Strongly Disagree

12. Teenagers who drop out of school tend to get into trouble in the community.

( ) Strongly Agree

( ) Agree

( ) Neutral

( ) Disagree

( ) Strongly Disagree

13. It is easy for teenagers in our community to buy alcohol.

( ) Strongly Agree

( ) Agree

( ) Neutral

( ) Disagree

( ) Strongly Disagree

14. Gangs are becoming a problem in our community.
    ( ) Strongly Agree
    ( ) Agree
    ( ) Neutral
    ( ) Disagree
    ( ) Strongly Disagree

15. Teenagers who drop out of school do not have the proper educational skills to obtain
    high-skill and high-paying jobs, thus costing employers more money to train these workers.
    ( ) Strongly Agree
    ( ) Agree
    ( ) Neutral
    ( ) Disagree
    ( ) Strongly Disagree

16. The school district in a community needs to find creative ways and programs to keep
    students motivated to remain in school and graduate.
    ( ) Strongly Agree
    ( ) Agree
    ( ) Neutral
    ( ) Disagree
    ( ) Strongly Disagree

17. Parents need to take an active role and be involved in their child's education and school
    as a good role model for their child.
    ( ) Strongly Agree
    ( ) Agree
    ( ) Neutral
    ( ) Disagree
    ( ) Strongly Disagree

18. Parents should be held responsible and accountable for making their child attend school each day.
    ( ) Strongly Agree
    ( ) Agree
    ( ) Neutral
    ( ) Disagree
    ( ) Strongly Disagree

19. Community members, the school district, businesses, churches, and social organizations and
    agencies should collaborate with each other to provide for children and families in need in the
    community.
    ( ) Strongly Agree
    ( ) Agree
    ( ) Neutral
    ( ) Disagree
    ( ) Strongly Disagree

20. Teenagers who drop out of school are usually bored and unmotivated by traditional teaching
    styles and instruction.
    ( ) Strongly Agree
    ( ) Agree
    ( ) Neutral
    ( ) Disagree
    ( ) Strongly Disagree

21. Tracking children in low, average, and high classes leads to low self-esteem and frustration for children placed in the low classes.
    ( ) Strongly Agree
    ( ) Agree
    ( ) Neutral
    ( ) Disagree
    ( ) Strongly Disagree

22. Alternative educational programs and schools that include parent, students, and staff working together to make learning interesting, fun, and motivating are needed in our community.
    ( ) Strongly Agree
    ( ) Agree
    ( ) Neutral
    ( ) Disagree
    ( ) Strongly Disagree

23. Vandalism, gangs, and violence will decrease if teenagers and their parents are actively involved in the school and community programs and activities.
    ( ) Strongly Agree
    ( ) Agree
    ( ) Neutral
    ( ) Disagree
    ( ) Strongly Disagree

24. Children need to relate real-life experiences to the academic information they learn in school to prepare and motivate them for life after graduation.
    ( ) Strongly Agree
    ( ) Agree
    ( ) Neutral
    ( ) Disagree
    ( ) Strongly Disagree

25. With the pressures, problems, and breakup of the traditional family in today's society, the schools should teach Character Education Values and organize Community Service projects for the students to teach them to "give back" to their community.
    ( ) Strongly Agree
    ( ) Agree
    ( ) Neutral
    ( ) Disagree
    ( ) Strongly Disagree

26. People feel like "winners" when they receive their high school diploma.
    ( ) Strongly Agree
    ( ) Agree
    ( ) Neutral
    ( ) Disagree
    ( ) Strongly Disagree

AT-RISK STUDENT IDENTIFICATION
AND TEACHER REFERRAL

Student's Name: _____ Referral Date: _____

Current Grade: _____ Current School: _____

Referring Teacher: _____ Counselor: _____ Admin: _____

Current Academic Information:

1. **Current Grades:**

   English   _____

   Math   _____

   Science   _____

   Social Studies _____

   Other   _____

   _____

2. **Standardized Test Scores**

   Reading   _____

   English   _____

   Science   _____

   Social Studies _____

3. **Student IQ**   _____

Current Behavioral Information:

Number of in-school suspensions year to date: _____

Major reasons: _____

Number of out-of-school suspensions year to date: _____

Major reasons: _____

PLEASE CHECK (✓) ALL APPLICABLE FACTORS IN EACH AREA BELOW THAT YOU FEEL PERTAIN TO THE STUDENT YOU ARE REFERRING.

Attendance Concerns

_____ Excessive absenteeism

_____ Excessive tardiness

_____ Excessive unexcused absences

_____ Excessive excused absences

_____ Parents do not call school for child's absences

_____ Parents do not make student attend school regularly

_____ Excessive truancies

_____ Often leaves school without permission

_____ Skips classes

Academic Concerns

_____ Receives Special Education Services

_____ Learning Disabilities

_____ Behavior Disorders

_____ Placed in Remedial Classes

_____ One or more years of grade-level retentions

_____ Currently failing grades in two or more courses

_____ Failed required English, math, science, or social studies

_____ Steadily declining grades over one or more years

_____ Underachiever/low effort

_____ Low achiever/high ability

_____ Low achiever/low ability

Social and Behavioral Concerns

_____ Disorganized

_____ Short attention span

_____ Defiant toward authority

_____ Cheats on homework, tests, or in games

_____ Displays refusal behaviors

_____ Aggressive or violent behavior toward people

_____ Low self-esteem

_____ Can't or won't accept responsibility for personal actions

_____ Displays inappropriate social skills or humor

_____ Apathy toward school

_____ Distractibility

_____ Steals

_____ Gets into physical fights

_____ Intimidates or bullies peers

_____ Withdrawn

_____ Throws objects or destroys school property when angry

_____ Dependent on peer group

_____ Easily influenced by peers

_____ Needs to be the center of attraction

_____ Afraid to try new things

_____ Exhibits sexually acting out behavior

_____ Repeated in-school suspensions

_____ Repeated out-of-school suspensions

_____ Frequently disrupts instruction

_____ Passive-resistant behavior

_____ Fear of failure

_____ Gets stressed easily

_____ Easily victimized

_____ Verbally abuses peers

_____ Threatens to harm staff

Health Concerns

_____ Diagnosed ADD

_____ Currently taking medication for ADD

_____ Diagnosed depression

_____ Currently taking medication for depression

_____ Suspicion of drug or alcohol abuse

_____ Has been under stress or in psychiatric hospital

_____ Diagnosed eating disorder

_____ Suspicion of eating disorder

_____ Appears tired or lethargic

_____ Is pregnant

_____ Noticeable change in hygiene

_____ Noticeable change in dress

_____ Noticeable change in weight

_____ Slurred speech

_____ Falls asleep easily in class

_____ Gets sick easily

_____ Physical handicap

Family Concerns

_____ Low socioeconomic status

_____ Middle socioeconomic status

_____ High socioeconomic status

_____ One or both parents graduated high school

_____ Single-parent household

_____ Stepparent household

_____ Lives with relatives

_____ Lives in foster home

_____ Lives on own

_____ Is a teenage parent

_____ Student helps financially support the family

STUDENT APPLICATION

Name: _____ Date: _____ Current Grade: _____

Address: _____ Phone: _____

_____ Birth Date: _____

Referred By: _____ Social Security Number: _____

THIS IS THE FIRST STEP OF THE APPLICATION AND THE ENROLLMENT PROCESS TO AT-
TEND THIS SCHOOL. PLEASE ANSWER EACH QUESTION HONESTLY, SERIOUSLY, AND IN
GREAT DETAIL. THE ENTIRE STAFF DISCUSSES AND REVIEWS **EACH** ANSWER YOU GIVE
TO DETERMINE IF OUR SCHOOL MIGHT SUIT YOUR NEEDS. THE INFORMATION YOU PRO-
VIDE ON THIS APPLICATION WILL DETERMINE IF YOU WILL PROCEED TO THE SECOND
STEP, WHICH IS AN INTERVIEW WITH ONE OR BOTH PARENTS WITH OUR STAFF. WE WILL
NOTIFY YOU WITHIN ONE WEEK OF RECEIVING THIS APPLICATION AS TO YOUR STATUS
IN THE ENROLLMENT PROCESS.

1. How important is it to you to graduate from high school?
   ( ) Very important
   ( ) Important
   ( ) Not too important

2. What are your career goals after high school?

   _____

   _____

3. Do you plan on attending one of the following after high school graduation?
   ( ) 2-year college
   ( ) Vocational technical school
   ( ) 4-year college
   ( ) Military service
   ( ) Work full-time

4. How do you learn best? (check all that fit your learning style)
   ( ) Lecture-style class
   ( ) Hands-on projects
   ( ) Computers
   ( ) Independent study courses

5. Why do you think this school will help you succeed in school?

   _____

   _____

6. How would you rate your attendance?
   ( ) Good—missed less than 2 days per semester
   ( ) Average—missed 3 to 5 days per semester
   ( ) Fair—missed 7 to 10 days per semester
   ( ) Poor—missed more than 10 days per semester

7. What do you value most about:

Yourself: _____

Your parents: _____

Your best friend: _____

Your favorite teacher: _____

8. What are your talents and strengths?

1. _____

2. _____

3. _____

9. What don't you like about your personality?

_____

_____

10. What are your academic weak areas?

_____

_____

11. What are your academic strength areas?

_____

_____

12. Name your three favorite leisure-time activities:

1. _____

2. _____

3. _____

13. Do you view yourself as being smart? Why or why not?

_____

_____

14. What would motivate you to do your best at school?

_____

_____

_____

15. How important to you is having a teacher really know you as a person? Why?

_____

_____

_____

16. Think of teachers that you've had in elementary school, middle school, or high school that
    you have really liked and had a good relationship with. Describe what made you like them.

    _____

    _____

    _____

    _____

17. You have been told that you have to show a commitment to yourself, the staff, and school if you
    are accepted as a student in this school. Explain how you will show your commitment to yourself,
    the staff, and our school if you become a student here.

    _____

    _____

    _____

    _____

18. Why do you feel we should accept you as a student at this school?

    _____

    _____

    _____

    _____

TENTATIVE ACCEPTANCE LETTER
FOR FIRST-YEAR STUDENT

Date: _____

Re: Student Name: _____

Dear Parents:

Your child has applied for enrollment at the Accelerated Alternative School for the _____ school year. The staff has reviewed your child's past grades, attendance, and any Misconducts your child has received at his/her current school, along with teacher, counselor, and administrator referral information. We have decided that this school may be a good place for your child to perform up to his/her intellectual abilities.

The second phase of the enrollment process is an INTERVIEW with the principal and several staff members at the Accelerated Alternative School. Parents are required to accompany the student to the interview. This is a good time for us to answer any questions you, the parent, may have concerning the Accelerated Alternative School and our programs. You and your child will be given a tour of the school and a Student Handbook during the interview. You will be notified at the interview or no later than 3 days after the interview whether your child has been officially accepted at this school for the next semester.

We only have a limited number of available enrollment slots for the next semester, so it is extremely important that you call our secretary as soon as possible to schedule your interview. If we do not hear from you by _____, we will take your child's name off the enrollment list and move on to the next name.

We look forward to working with you and your child. The Accelerated Alternative School is a unique alternative school for students with average to superior intelligence but who are not working up to their capabilities at the traditional school. We are a part of Dr. Henry Levin's National Accelerated Schools Program, which involves creating a truly collaborative school with the input and help of the students, parents, and staff. Our courses are not remedial in nature but rather are accelerated, using computers, Off-Site-Experiences, Community Service, and Powerful Learning Experiences to deliver the academic information. The parents, students, and staff work side by side to create our "Dream School."

We look forward to meeting with you and your child at the interview session.

Sincerely,

The Principal

Carrie Baylard Eidson and Edward D. Hillhouse, *The Accelerated High School: A Step-by-Step Guide for Administrators and Teachers.* Copyright © 1998 by Corwin Press, Inc.

WAITING LIST STATUS

Date: _____

Student Name: _____

Dear Parents:

Your child, _____, has applied to be a student at the Accelerated Alternative School for the _____ school year. We are pleased that your child has expressed an interest in attending our school.

We are sorry to inform you that at this time we do not have any available enrollment slots in your child's upcoming grade level for the fall semester. Your child is number _____ on the **Waiting List** for the _____ grade level. We will call you as the space becomes available.

Thank you again for your interest in our school.

Sincerely,

The Principal

NONACCEPTANCE OF STUDENT

Date: _____

Student Name: _____

Dear Parents:

Your child, _____, has applied to attend the Accelerated Alternative School for the _____ school year. The staff has reviewed your child's academic records, reading ability, attendance, attitude, behavior, and misconducts from his/her current school to determine if the Accelerated Alternative School would be a good educational placement for your child.

Unfortunately, after completing our review of records and referral information we do not feel this school would be beneficial for your child. **We will not be able to enroll your child at the Accelerated Alternative School for the following reasons:**

1. _____

2. _____

3. _____

4. _____

5. _____

Sincerely,

The Principal

PARENT COMMITMENT CONTRACT

The following statements identify the commitment that you as the parent must display to the Accelerated Alternative School and your child in order for your child to be a student at this school. Parent commitment and involvement is an extremely important and necessary part of a successful school and good role modeling for your child. Please read this contract carefully. Sign this contract if you are truly sincere and are willing and able to commit yourself and be involved with your child, the staff, and this school. If this commitment contract is not honored, your child will be dismissed from this school.

1. I pledge to be an involved parent in my child's education. My goal is to help my child persevere and do his/her best in school in order to graduate from high school.

2. I understand that this is an Accelerated School, and I have the opportunity to get involved in the decision making in all aspects of this school by serving on cadres.

3. I promise to work on a specific cadre and attend one meeting per month to work on challenge areas and procedures pertaining to the cadre I join.

4. I promise to encourage my child to strive to use his/her high intelligence, abilities, and talents to gain a deep knowledge from the academic courses.

5. I promise to attend the Fall Parent-Teacher Conference and the Spring Parent-Teacher Conference to discuss my child's academic and social progress.

6. I promise to make sure my child attends school regularly.

7. I will only call my child "in sick" if my child is truly sick. I will not enable my child to miss school by giving him/her a fake alibi.

8. I will support the Discipline Code of the school and the consequences for my child if he/she breaks the rules.

9. I understand that if my child does not show commitment to this school through attitude, behavior, and academic progress, my child will be put on Probation. If my child does not meet the conditions for Probation, my child will be dismissed from this school.

10. I will not hesitate to call the school if I have any ideas, concerns, or suggestions to help my child or the school succeed.

I have read this contract and agree to follow each of the points to the very best of my ability. I understand that if I cannot fulfill my commitment, then my child will be dismissed from this school.

Parent Signature: _____ Date: _____

STUDENT COMMITMENT CONTRACT

The following statements identify the commitment that you must have and show to yourself, the staff, and the other students at this school. Please read this contract carefully. Sign this contract if you are truly sincere about your commitment to our school. This signed contract is proof of your commitment to the staff and students at this school. If you do not fulfill this contract on a consistent basis, you will be dismissed from this school.

1. I agree to use my intellectual potential to the fullest by trying my hardest in each course I take.
2. I will use my talents to solve problems and give input in class discussions and projects.
3. I will be open to trying new ideas, activities, and challenges.
4. I will keep my attitude positive and try not to complain unjustifiably.
5. I understand attending school regularly is a major requirement at this school. I promise come to school even when I don't feel like it.
6. I promise to miss school only if I am truly sick. I will not have my parents "call in sick" for me unless I am truly sick.
7. I promise to show respect and talk respectfully to the staff and other students at all times.
8. I promise to come prepared to class with all the necessary materials and work.
9. I will follow classroom and school rules at all times.
10. I understand that this is an Accelerated Alternative School, which means that I will be given the opportunities to give input, ideas, and suggestions to improve the school and plan student activities, courses, and discipline rules. I promise to be involved in making this school a "family" and a "community" of belonging and acceptance for all.
11. I will participate fully in Community Service Learning Projects and Off-Site Experiences without complaining.
12. I promise not to skip school on Community Service Days, Off-Site Experience Days, Field Days, etc. I know attending and participating in these days shows Unity of Purpose and helps make our school family closer.
13. I will seek help from staff members when I have a problem of any kind. I will not let a small problem become a large, overwhelming problem.
14. I will take responsibility for my own behavior and learning. I will not blame my parents, staff, or other students for my actions.

I have read this contract and agree to follow each of the points to the very best of my ability. I understand that continued violation of this contract will be cause for my dismissal from this school.

Student Signature: _____   Date: _____

Carrie Baylard Eidson and Edward D. Hillhouse, *The Accelerated High School: A Step-by-Step Guide for Administrators and Teachers.* Copyright © 1998 by Corwin Press, Inc.

READMISSION APPLICATION AND
STUDENT REFLECTIONS FOR FALL SEMESTER

Student Name: _____ Date: _____

YOU HAVE BEEN A STUDENT AT THIS SCHOOL DURING THIS SCHOOL YEAR. ALL STU-
DENTS MUST REAPPLY FOR ADMISSION TO THIS SCHOOL EACH YEAR. PLEASE ANSWER
THE FOLLOWING QUESTIONS SERIOUSLY AND COMPLETELY. THE STAFF WILL BE READ-
ING THESE AND USING YOUR ANSWERS AS PART OF THE EVALUATION PROCESS IN YOUR
REAPPLICATION TO COME BACK TO THIS SCHOOL IN THE FALL.

1. Why do you want to come back to this school in the fall?

    _____

    _____

2. How will you try to make this school a positive place for yourself and other students and staff?

    _____

    _____

3. What have you learned this year about "Empowerment with Responsibility"?

    _____

    _____

4. Describe to us what it means to be an Accelerated Alternative School such as we are.

    _____

    _____

5. What major goals are you working on for yourself right now?

    _____

    _____

6. How do you plan to show us that you are committed to this school and its rules and programs?

    _____

    _____

7. What changes in yourself have you noticed since being at this school?

    _____

    _____

    _____

8. Describe a major item or area in your behavior or personality that you feel gets in the way of you achieving at your best.

_____

_____

_____

9. What do you feel is your biggest strength and most interesting aspect of you as a person?

_____

_____

_____

10. Describe your plan as to how you will work positively through any problem you encounter at this school next year with friends, staff, rules, etc.

_____

_____

_____

11. How can you as a student at this school help other students become more responsible for their behavior?

_____

_____

_____

12. We like to pride ourselves at this school on having tolerance for differences in people. How will you show tolerance and acceptance to new students at this school?

_____

_____

_____

13. We always tell our students that this school is a "Privilege School." How will you show us that you will live up to this privilege?

_____

_____

_____

14. One of our goals is to create a positive image of this school in this community. How will you help us create this positive image as a student in this school?

_____

_____

_____

ACCEPTANCE LETTER FOR READMISSION AS
A CONTINUING STUDENT FOR FALL _____

Date: _____

Student Name: _____

Dear Parents:

Your child, _____, has applied to return to the Accelerated Alternative School in the fall. After reviewing his/her Readmission Application, grades, attitude, and commitment to our program this year, our staff is happy to inform you that _____, **has been accepted** as a student at this school again for the next school year.

We have enjoyed having your child with us this year and we are looking forward to working with you and your family next fall. Registration will be held the week of _____. Students may pick up their schedules at the time they register.

Have a wonderful, relaxing, and fun summer!

Sincerely,

The Principal

STUDENT GOVERNANCE CADRE STAFF REFERRAL

Student Name: _____ Date: _____

Presenting Problem: _____

_____

_____

_____

_____

_____

_____

_____

Is this student already on Official Probation? _____

Have the parents been contacted by staff members? _____

    Contact dates: _____ _____ _____ _____

    Results: _____

_____

Staff Signatures:

_____   _____

_____   _____

_____   _____

_____   _____

_____   _____

_____   _____

STUDENT GOVERNANCE CADRE ACTION PLAN

Student Name: _____ Date: _____

Initial Action Plan _____ Revised Action Plan _____

Goals:

  1. _____

  2. _____

  3. _____

Objectives:

  1. _____

  2. _____

  3. _____

  4. _____

Strategies:

  1. _____

  2. _____

  3. _____

  4. _____

  5. _____

Date of Next Meeting: _____

(Copy this page for each week's charting)

STUDENT REFLECTION LOG

Student Name: _____   Start Date: _____

Date: Reflections of daily progress toward goals:

_____   _____

_____   _____

_____   _____

_____   _____

_____   _____

_____   _____

Personal rating of this week's progress:

Successes:

Pitfalls:

STUDENT GOVERNANCE CADRE PARENT NOTICE

Student Name: _____   Date: _____

Your child has been referred to the Student Governance Cadre for the following **behavior problems,** which are consistently violating the Commitment Contract he/she signed as a student in this school:

1. _____

2. _____

3. _____

4. _____

The Student Governance Cadre has recommended the following strategies to help your child decrease these behaviors and honor his/her Commitment Contract:

1. _____

2. _____

3. _____

4. _____

The Student Governance Cadre would like to meet with **you** and **your child** to review the progress your child is making toward meeting these goals.

Parent Conference Date: _____

Time: _____   Place: _____

Thank you for your commitment as a parent to your child's education and to this school. We look forward to meeting with you and your child on the above date.

Student Governance Cadre Members:

_____   _____

_____   _____

_____   _____

_____   _____

HOME COURT REVIEW

Date: _____

Dear Parents:

Your child, _____, has been referred to the Home Court Review by the Student Governance Cadre. Home Court Review is a serious matter that requires you and your child to appear before the entire staff on the following date: _____ Time: _____.

The Home Court Review is a mandatory meeting that follows weeks of intervention strategies and Action Plan goals developed by the Student Governance Cadre and your child to help your child improve his/her behavior, attitude, and/or grades at this school. Your child has been referred for a Home Court Review because the Student Governance Cadre did not see a consistent improvement and commitment from your child in working with the Action Plan interventions and strategies. Your child has not consistently fulfilled the promises he/she made when he/she read and signed the Student Commitment Contract.

The Home Court Review will determine the conditions your child will have to meet in order to remain at this school next semester. The Home Court Review will discuss the following areas of concern with you and your child at the meeting:

1. _____

2. _____

3. _____

4. _____

We look forward to meeting with you and having your support and input in helping your child fulfill his/her commitment to this school.

Sincerely,

The Principal

STUDENT PROBATION FOR _____ SCHOOL YEAR

Date: _____

Student Name: _____

Dear Parents:

Our staff has reviewed your child's grades, attitude, commitment, behavior, academic progress, attendance, Readmission Application, and other pertinent information that would help us decide if the Accelerated Alternative School is the best educational placement for your child for the upcoming school year.

You are aware from phone conversations and meetings with you concerning the areas your child is having difficulty with at our school. We have decided to accept your child back at the Accelerated Alternative School on **Probation** for the entire _____ school year. To remain at this school, your child must *consistently* meet the following conditions and will be reevaluated at the end of each semester.

CONDITIONS THAT MUST BE MET TO REMAIN AT THE ACCELERATED ALTERNATIVE SCHOOL:

1. _____

2. _____

3. _____

4. _____

Sincerely,

The Principal

HOME COURT REVIEW STUDENT PROBATION NOTICE

Student Name: _____ Date: _____

Presenting Problem:

_____

_____

_____

Discussion:

_____

_____

_____

_____

Conditions that must be met consistently to remain at this school:

1. _____

2. _____

3. _____

4. _____

Signatures of Home Court Review Members, Parent(s), and student:

_____   _____

_____   _____

_____   _____

OFFICIAL STUDENT DISMISSAL NOTICE

Date: _____

Student Name: _____

Dear Parents:

As you have been aware, your child has been on **Official Probation** since _____, for the following reasons:

1. _____

2. _____

3. _____

4. _____

Our entire staff has reviewed your child's progress in remediating the concerns listed above. It is our decision that this program is not the proper placement for your child at this time. Therefore your child will be **dismissed** from the Accelerated Alternative School at the end of this semester.

Sincerely,

The Principal

INQUIRY PROCESS

Name: _____ Date: _____ Grade: _____

Problem or Challenge Area:

_____

_____

_____

_____

_____

_____

Possible Causes:

_____

_____

_____

_____

_____

_____

_____

_____

Possible Solutions:

_____

_____

_____

_____

_____

_____

_____

ACTION PLAN

Name: _____ Date: _____ Grade: _____

Unit or Project Title: _____

Goal(s):

_____

_____

_____

_____

Objectives:

_____

_____

_____

_____

Activities:

_____

_____

_____

_____

Timeline and Provider:

_____

_____

Evaluation Activity:

_____

_____

_____

_____

ACTION PLAN REFLECTIONS AND EVALUATION

Name: _____ Date: _____ Grade: _____

Unit Number and Title: _____

Unit Goals:

_____

_____

How did your group achieve its goal?

_____

_____

_____

Explain why you feel the action plan did work or did not work in helping your group achieve the action plan goal:

_____

_____

_____

Did your group's action plan use the three principles of accelerated schools? how? Give examples for each principle:

_____

_____

_____

_____

Unity of Purpose:

_____

_____

Empowerment With Responsibility:

_____

_____

Building on Strengths:

_____

_____

_____

Describe the powerful learning experiences the action plan had you participate in with this project:

_____

_____

_____

How did *you personally* experience empowerment with responsibility from participating in this project?

_____

_____

_____

What did you learn about yourself from participating in this project?

_____

_____

_____

What did you learn about other people from participating in this project?

_____

_____

_____

Teacher's Comments:

_____

_____

_____

Principal's Comments:

_____

_____

_____

ACCELERATED ALTERNATIVE SCHOOL/
CARING COMMUNITIES STEERING COMMITTEE
CADRE MONITORING FORM

Cadre Name: _____ Date: _____

Goal(s):	Date:	Progressing/Met:
_____	_____	_____
_____	_____	_____
_____	_____	_____
_____	_____	_____
_____	_____	_____

Strategies:	Date:	Progress/Completed:
_____	_____	_____
_____	_____	_____
_____	_____	_____
_____	_____	_____

Evaluation Results:

_____

_____

_____

_____

_____

_____

_____

_____

_____

_____

_____

CADRE ACTION PLAN

Cadre Name: _____ Starting Date: _____

Revision Date: _____   Ending Date: _____

Presenting Problem:

_____

_____

Baseline Data:

_____

_____

Goal:

_____

_____

Strategies: Timeline: Provider:

_____   _____   _____

_____   _____   _____

_____   _____   _____

_____   _____   _____

Evaluation Activities:

_____

_____

Results:

_____

_____

Cadre Members' Signatures:

_____   _____   _____

_____   _____   _____

_____   _____   _____

CARING COMMUNITIES FAMILY PLAN

Family Name: _____ Date: _____

Address: _____ Phone: _____

_____ Zip Code: _____

Mother: _____ Age: _____   Father: _____ Age: _____
_____   _____

Children: _____ Ages: _____   Children: _____ Ages: _____
_____   _____

_____   _____

_____   _____

Case Manager: _____

Presenting Problem:
_____

_____

Goal:
_____

_____

Strategies: Provider: Timeline:
_____   _____   _____

_____   _____   _____

_____   _____   _____

Progress Report or Conclusion:
_____

_____

Steering Committee Members' Signatures:

_____   _____   _____

_____   _____   _____

_____   _____   _____

END-OF-THE-YEAR PARENT PROGRAM EVALUATION

School Year _____

To help us evaluate how our program at the Accelerated Alternative School is progressing and to get your input on different matters, please fill out this survey evaluation. We have enclosed a stamped, self-addressed envelope for your convenience. Thank you for your help and input in the continual growth and development of our "Dream School." Please place a check mark (✓) next to the answer that best describes your feelings concerning our school.

The Staff

Accelerated Alternative School

1. Since attending this Accelerated Alternative School, my child's attitude toward school has become:
   ( ) Positive
   ( ) Stayed the same
   ( ) Negative

2. My child seems to be motivated by the hands-on experiences provided at this school.
   ( ) Strongly Agree
   ( ) Agree
   ( ) Neutral
   ( ) Disagree
   ( ) Strongly Disagree

3. My child likes using the computers as an instructional tool.
   ( ) Strongly Agree
   ( ) Agree
   ( ) Neutral
   ( ) Disagree
   ( ) Strongly Disagree

4. I feel the course and subject matter at this school are just as rigorous as those at the traditional high school or middle school.
   ( ) Strongly Agree
   ( ) Agree
   ( ) Neutral
   ( ) Disagree
   ( ) Strongly Disagree

5. I like the Community Service aspect of the curriculum.
   ( ) Strongly Agree
   ( ) Agree
   ( ) Neutral
   ( ) Disagree
   ( ) Strongly Disagree

Carrie Baylard Eidson and Edward D. Hillhouse, *The Accelerated High School: A Step-by-Step Guide for Administrators and Teachers.* Copyright © 1998 by Corwin Press, Inc.

6. My child has more confidence in his/her academic ability since attending this school.
   - ( ) Strongly Agree
   - ( ) Agree
   - ( ) Neutral
   - ( ) Disagree
   - ( ) Strongly Disagree

7. My child's self-esteem has risen since attending this school.
   - ( ) Strongly Agree
   - ( ) Agree
   - ( ) Neutral
   - ( ) Disagree
   - ( ) Strongly Disagree

8. Communication between staff and parents concerning student academic progress, behavior, and events is satisfactory.
   - ( ) Strongly Agree
   - ( ) Agree
   - ( ) Neutral
   - ( ) Disagree
   - ( ) Strongly Disagree

9. I like having the Family Leader send me postcards or telephone me every 2 weeks with updates on my child's progress.
   - ( ) Strongly Agree
   - ( ) Agree
   - ( ) Neutral
   - ( ) Disagree
   - ( ) Strongly Disagree

10. I feel that I do have the opportunity to provide input into this school through the availability of being on a school cadre if I choose.
    - ( ) Strongly Agree
    - ( ) Agree
    - ( ) Neutral
    - ( ) Disagree
    - ( ) Strongly Disagree

11. I want this school to continue to be a part of the National Accelerated Schools Program, which allows and welcomes input and involvement of parents, staff, and students.
    - ( ) Strongly Agree
    - ( ) Agree
    - ( ) Neutral
    - ( ) Disagree
    - ( ) Strongly Disagree

12. I like "Saturday School" as an alternative option to out-of-school suspension.
    - ( ) Strongly Agree
    - ( ) Agree
    - ( ) Neutral
    - ( ) Disagree
    - ( ) Strongly Disagree

13. This school's atmosphere is warm and friendly.
   ( ) Strongly Agree
   ( ) Agree
   ( ) Neutral
   ( ) Disagree
   ( ) Strongly Disagree

14. I feel my child has improved academically at this Accelerated Alternative School.
   ( ) Strongly Agree
   ( ) Agree
   ( ) Neutral
   ( ) Disagree
   ( ) Strongly Disagree

15. My child is challenged by the subjects and material offered at this school.
   ( ) Strongly Agree
   ( ) Agree
   ( ) Neutral
   ( ) Disagree
   ( ) Strongly Disagree

16. My child feels accepted and has a sense of belonging at this school.
   ( ) Strongly Agree
   ( ) Agree
   ( ) Neutral
   ( ) Disagree
   ( ) Strongly Disagree

17. I believe the student-teacher relationship is the key to having a successful, accepting, and caring school community.
   ( ) Strongly Agree
   ( ) Agree
   ( ) Neutral
   ( ) Disagree
   ( ) Strongly Disagree

18. I feel this school has followed the Vision for this school that was written by parents, students, and staff and published in the Handbook.
   ( ) Strongly Agree
   ( ) Agree
   ( ) Neutral
   ( ) Disagree
   ( ) Strongly Disagree

19. I feel there is a Unity of Purpose among the staff, students, and parents at this school.
   ( ) Strongly Agree
   ( ) Agree
   ( ) Neutral
   ( ) Disagree
   ( ) Strongly Disagree

20. I like the school's emphasis on academic excellence and the grading system of "A, B, C, Incomplete," instead of having D and F.
    ( ) Strongly Agree
    ( ) Agree
    ( ) Neutral
    ( ) Disagree
    ( ) Strongly Disagree

21. Please list some events or activities that the school could provide that would get parents motivated to become involved in this school:
    1. _____
    2. _____
    3. _____
    4. _____

22. What other services would you like to see this school provide for your child and family?
    1. _____
    2. _____
    3. _____

23. What talents or hobbies can you share with our students on a "Club Day"?
    1. _____
    2. _____

END-OF-THE-YEAR
STUDENT PROGRAM EVALUATION

To continually improve our school to meet the academic and social needs of our students, we need input, ideas, and suggestions from each student. Please help us evaluate our school procedures, policies, and programs by honestly and seriously answering each question below and on the following pages. Please place a check mark (✓) by the answer that best represents how you feel about the information asked.

Thank you for your help in creating our "Dream School."

Your Staff

1. Since attending this school, my attitude toward school has
   ( ) Changed positively
   ( ) Remained apathetic
   ( ) Changed negatively

2. Since attending this school, my attendance has
   ( ) Improved
   ( ) Remained unchanged
   ( ) Became worse

3. The Accelerated Schools Principle of *Unity of Purpose* means
   ( ) Every student does his/her own thing academically.
   ( ) Staff, students, and parents work together toward a common goal.
   ( ) The staff makes all the decisions pertaining to the school.

4. I am motivated by opportunities for hands-on experiences and projects.
   ( ) Strongly Agree
   ( ) Agree
   ( ) Neutral
   ( ) Disagree
   ( ) Strongly Agree

5. I like using computers as an instructional tool.
   ( ) Strongly Agree
   ( ) Agree
   ( ) Neutral
   ( ) Disagree
   ( ) Strongly Disagree

6. I feel better about my academic abilities since attending this school.
   ( ) Strongly Agree
   ( ) Agree
   ( ) Neutral
   ( ) Disagree
   ( ) Strongly Disagree

7. I feel the students have the opportunities to decide how they will show they have mastered an academic concept or skill.
   ( ) Strongly Agree
   ( ) Agree
   ( ) Neutral
   ( ) Disagree
   ( ) Strongly Disagree

8. I like being able to show that I understand an academic concept or skill by (Check *all* that apply to you):
   ( ) Tests
   ( ) Writing reports or summaries
   ( ) Making something from different materials to demonstrate the concept
   ( ) Using art mediums such as murals, posters, etc.
   ( ) Videotaping what I have learned
   ( ) Writing and performing a play about the concept
   ( ) Other _____

9. I feel the course and subject matter at this school are just as rigorous as those at the traditional high school or middle school.
   ( ) Strongly Agree
   ( ) Agree
   ( ) Neutral
   ( ) Disagree
   ( ) Strongly Disagree

10. I like the Community Service aspect of the curriculum.
    ( ) Strongly Agree
    ( ) Agree
    ( ) Neutral
    ( ) Disagree
    ( ) Strongly Disagree

11. The Accelerated Schools Principle of *Empowerment with Responsibility* means
    ( ) Freedom to do what I want no matter what
    ( ) Freedom to make decisions and being responsible for them
    ( ) Acting responsible, with the power to give input, ideas, and suggestions to change and improve the school

12. I feel accepted and have a sense of belonging at this school.
    ( ) Strongly Agree
    ( ) Agree
    ( ) Neutral
    ( ) Disagree
    ( ) Strongly Disagree

13. I feel that the staff really listens to me as a person.
    ( ) Strongly Agree
    ( ) Agree
    ( ) Neutral
    ( ) Disagree
    ( ) Strongly Disagree

14. The Accelerated Schools Principle of *Building on Strengths* means
    ( ) Combining my talents and strength areas to help make our "Dream School" or academic projects
    ( ) Combining the talents and strengths of the staff, students, and parents to create our "Dream School"
    ( ) Combining my talents and strengths with small groups or a partner to demonstrate mastery of an academic concept or skill
    ( ) All of the above

15. I like having a "Family Group" and "Family Leader."
    ( ) Strongly Agree
    ( ) Agree
    ( ) Neutral
    ( ) Disagree
    ( ) Strongly Disagree

16. I feel I have the opportunity to provide input into this school through being on a cadre.
    ( ) Strongly Agree
    ( ) Agree
    ( ) Neutral
    ( ) Disagree
    ( ) Strongly Disagree

17. This school's atmosphere is warm, friendly, and fun.
    ( ) Strongly Agree
    ( ) Agree
    ( ) Neutral
    ( ) Disagree
    ( ) Strongly Disagree

18. I feel we need more Off-Site-Experiences during the school year.
    ( ) Strongly Agree
    ( ) Agree
    ( ) Neutral
    ( ) Disagree
    ( ) Strongly Disagree

19. I would like to have intramural sports and tournaments at this school.
    ( ) Strongly Agree
    ( ) Agree
    ( ) Neutral
    ( ) Disagree
    ( ) Strongly Disagree

20. List three (3) clubs you would like to have at this school on "Club Day" next school year:
    1. _____
    2. _____
    3. _____

21. I feel Conflict Mediation is effective in solving student problems.
    ( ) Strongly Agree
    ( ) Agree

( ) Neutral
( ) Disagree
( ) Strongly Disagree

22. I like the "A, B, C, Incomplete" grading system.

    ( ) Strongly Agree
    ( ) Agree
    ( ) Neutral
    ( ) Disagree
    ( ) Strongly Disagree

23. I like the Block Schedule we presently have at this school.

    ( ) Strongly Agree
    ( ) Agree
    ( ) Neutral
    ( ) Disagree
    ( ) Strongly Disagree

24. How important is it to you to have a genuine, close student-teacher relationship?

    ( ) Very Important
    ( ) Important
    ( ) Not Important

25. The staff shows genuine commitment to the students and this school.

    ( ) Strongly Agree
    ( ) Agree
    ( ) Neutral
    ( ) Disagree
    ( ) Strongly Disagree

26. I feel the students are given *Empowerment with Responsibility* in important decisions pertaining to discipline, procedures, assemblies, and Community Service projects.

    ( ) Strongly Agree
    ( ) Agree
    ( ) Neutral
    ( ) Disagree
    ( ) Strongly Disagree

27. I feel there is a *Unity of Purpose* among the staff, students, and parents at this school.

    ( ) Strongly Agree
    ( ) Agree
    ( ) Neutral
    ( ) Disagree
    ( ) Strongly Disagree

28. Name three (3) things you would like to see changed at this school.

    1. _____

    2. _____

    3. _____

29. On a scale of 1 to 10, with 10 being the highest, how would you rate this school? (Circle your choice.)

    1 2 3 4 5 6 7 8 9 10

References

Armstrong, T. (1994). *Multiple intelligences in the classroom.* Alexandria, VA: Association for Supervision and Curriculum Development.

Arnove, R. F., & Strout, T. (1980). Alternative schools for disruptive youth. *The Educational Forum, 44*(4), 452-471.

Barber, L. W., & McCellan, M. C. (1987). Looking at America's dropouts. *Phi Delta Kappan, 69,* 264-267.

Barr, R. D., & Parrett, W. H. (1997). *How to create alternative, magnet, and charter schools that work.* Bloomington, IN: National Educational Service.

Barth, R. (1990). *Improving schools from within.* San Francisco: Jossey-Bass.

Baum, S. M., Renzulli, J. S., & Hebert, T. P. (1994, November). Reversing underachievement: Stories of success. *Educational Leadership, 52*(3), 48-52.

Bennett, T. (1997). *Connections project.* William Woods University, Fulton, MO.

Bennis, W., & Nanus, B. (1985). *Leaders: The strategies for taking charge.* New York: Harper & Row.

Brendtro, L. K., Brokenleg, M., & Van Bockern, S. (1990). *Reclaiming youth at risk: Our hope for the future.* Bloomington, IN: National Educational Service.

Brooks, R. (1980). Gifted delinquents. *Educational Research, 22*(3), 212-220.

Buck-Collopy, R., & Green, T. (1995, September). Using motivational theory with at-risk children. *Educational Leadership, 53*(1), 37-40.

Canfield, J. (1990, September). Improving students' self-esteem. *Educational Leadership, 48*(1), 48-50.

Capuzzi, D., & Gross, D. (Eds.). (1996). *Youth at risk: A prevention resource for counselors, teachers, and parents* (2nd ed.). Alexandria, VA: American Counseling Association.

Clifford, M. M. (1990). Students need challenge, not easy success. *Educational Leadership, 48*(1), 22-25.

Clinton, Bill. (1997, February 4). State of the union address [Conference handout]. U.S. Department of Education, Secretary's Regional Representative Region VII, Kansas City, MO.

Cummins, J. (1992). The empowerment of Indian students. In J. Reyhner (Ed.), *Teaching American Indian students* (pp. 4-5). Norman: University of Oklahoma Press.

Davis, J. K., & Cochran, K. F. (1989). An information processing view of field dependence-independence. *Early Child Development and Care, 43,* 129-145.

Deblois, R. (1989). Keeping at risk students in school: Toward a curriculum for potential dropouts. *NASSP Bulletin, 73,* 6-12.

DuFour, R., & Eaker, R. (1992). *Creating the new American school: A principal's guide to school improvement.* Bloomington, IN: National Educational Service.

Durkeen, J. H. (1981). *Secondary school dropouts.* St. Paul: Minnesota State Department of Education.

Dwyer, D. C. (1984, February). The search for instructional leadership: Routines and subtleties in the principal's role. *Educational Leadership, 41,* 32-37.

Edmonds, R. R. (1982, December). Programs of school improvement: An overview. *Educational Leadership, 40,* 4-11.

Eidson, C. B., & Hillhouse, E. D. (1997). *Building a Caring Community through Community Service Learning: A curriculum for 8th-12th grade.* Unpublished manuscript.

Ekstrom, R. E., Goertz, M. E., Pollack, J. M., & Rock, D. A. (1986). Who drops out of school and why: Findings from a national study. *Teachers College Record, 87,* 356-373.

Farrell, E. (1990). *Hanging in and dropping out: Voices of at risk high school students.* New York: Teachers College Press.

Finnan, C., McCarthy, J., St. John, E., & Slovacek, S. (1995). *Accelerated schools in action: Lessons from the field.* Thousand Oaks, CA: Corwin, 1995.

Firestone, W. A., & Rosenblum, S. (1988). Building commitment in urban high schools. *Educational Evaluation and Policy Analysis, 4,* 285-299.

Fitzhenry, R. I., (Ed.). (1993). *The Harper book of quotations* (3rd ed.). New York: Harper-Collins.

Gardner, H. (1983). *Frames of mind: The theory of multiple intelligences.* New York: Harper & Row.

Gipson, F. (1956). *Old Yeller.* New York: Scholastic.

Glasser, W. (1969). *Schools without failure.* New York: Harper & Row.

Goodlad, J. I. (1984). *A place called school.* New York: McGraw-Hill.

Goodman, K. (1986). *What's whole in whole language?* Portsmouth, NH: Heineman.

Grennon-Brooks, J., & Brooks, M. G. (1993). *In search of understanding: The case for constructivist classrooms.* Alexandria, VA: Association for Supervision and Curriculum Development.

Hinton, S. E. (1967). *The outsiders.* New York: Dell.

Hirschi, T. (1987). *Courses of delinquency.* Berkeley: University of California Press.

Hopfenberg, W. S., Levin, H. M., & Associates. (1993). *The accelerated schools resource guide.* San Francisco: Jossey-Bass.

Huck, C. (1977). Literature as the content of reading. *Theory Into Practice, 16,* 363—371.

Jackson, P. W. (1986). *The practice of teaching.* New York: Teachers College Press.

Jankowski, M. A. (1991). *Islands in the street: Gangs and American urban society.* Berkeley: University of California Press.

Johnson, J. A., Dupuis, V. L., Musial, D., Hall, G. E., & Gollnick, D. M. (1996). *Introduction to the foundations of American education.* Needham, MA: Allyn & Bacon.

Kellmayer, J. (1995). *How to establish an alternative school.* Thousand Oaks, CA: Corwin.

Kohn, A. (1996). *Beyond discipline.* Alexandria, VA: Association for Supervision and Curriculum Development.

Kozol, J. (1991). *Savage inequalities.* New York: Crown.

Lazear, D. (1991). *Seven ways of knowing: Teaching for multiple intelligences.* Palatine, IL: IRI/Skylight Publishing.

Lee, H. (1960). *To kill a mockingbird.* New York: Warner.

Levin, H. M. (1988). *Structuring schools for greater effectiveness with educationally disadvantaged or at-risk students.* Paper presented at the Annual Meeting of the American Educational Research Association, New Orleans.

Madden, N. A., & Slavin, R. (1989). What works for students at risk: A research synthesis. *Educational Research, 46*(2), 4-12.

McGowan, J. P. (1972). *Measurement and evaluation of immersion-type teaching in secondary schools versus the traditional teaching existent today: Final report.* Washington DC: National Center for Educational Research and Development.

McKenzie, B. K. (1992). A media education program for teachers of high-risk students. (Monograph). *Technology and Teacher Education Annual,* pp. 61-65. ISBN 1-880094-037

McWhirter, J. J., McWhirter, B., McWhirter, A., & McWhirter, E. (1993). *At-risk youth: A comprehensive response.* Pacific Grove, CA: Brooks/Cole.

Naisbitt, J., & Aburdene, P. (1985). *Reinventing the corporation.* New York: Warner.

Natriello, G., McDill, E. L., & Pallas, A. M. (1988). *In our lifetime: Schooling and the disadvantaged.* New York: Committee for Economic Development.

National Association for the Education of Young Children and the National Association of Early Childhood Specialists in State Departments of Education. (1991, March). Guidelines for appropriate curriculum content and assessment in programs serving children ages 3 through 8. *Young Children,* pp. 21-38.

National Association of Secondary School Principals & Carnegie Foundation. (1996). *Breaking ranks: Changing an American institution.* Reston, VA: National Association of Secondary School Principals.

Newman, J. (1985). *Whole language: Theory in use.* Portsmouth, NH: Heineman.

Osborne, J. K., & Brynes, D. A. (1990). Gifted, disaffected, disruptive youths and the alternative high school. *The Gifted Child Today, 13,* 45-48.

Peters, T. J., & Waterman, R. H., Jr. (1982). *In search of excellence: Lessons from America's best-run companies.* New York: Harper & Row.

Petras, K., & Petras, R., (Eds.). (1995). *The whole world book of quotations.* Reading, MA: Addison-Wesley.

Powell, B. S. (1976). *Intensive education: The impact of time on learning.* Newton, MA: Education Development Center.

Ralph, J. (1989). Improving education for the disadvantaged: Do we know whom to help? *Phi Delta Kappan, 70,* 393-400.

Rawls, W. (1961). *Where the red fern grows.* New York: Curtis.

Renzulli, J. S. (1994). *Schools for talent development: A practical plan for total school improvement.* Mansfield Center, CT: Creative Learning Press.

Sagor, R. (1996, September). Building resiliency in students. *Educational Leadership, 54*(1), 38-43.

Saracho, O. N., & Spodek, B. (1981). Teachers' cognitive styles: Educational implications. *The Educational Forum, 45,* 153-159.

Senge, P. (1990). *The fifth discipline: The art and practice of the learning organization.* New York: Doubleday Currency.

Sizer, T. (1992). *Horace's compromise: The dilemma of the American high school.* Boston: Houghton Mifflin.

Slavin, R. E. (1987, November). Cooperative learning and the cooperative school. *Educational Leadership, 45,* 7-13.

Solomon, G. (1993, October). Making a difference: Technology and the non-tracked classroom. *Electronic Learning, 13,* 18-19.

Warner, C. (with Curry, M.). (1997). *Everybody's house—The schoolhouse.* Thousand Oaks, CA: Corwin.

Waxman, H. C., Walker de Felix, J., Anderson, J. E., & Baptiste, H. P., Jr. (1992). *Students at risk in at risk schools.* Newbury Park, CA: Corwin.

Wehlage, G. G., Rutter, R. A., Smith, G. A., Lesko, M., & Fernandez, R. R. (1989). *Reducing the risk: Schools as communities of support.* New York: Falmer.

Wehlage, G. G., Rutter, R. A., & Turnbaugh, A. (1987). A program model for at risk high school students. *Educational Leadership, 44*(6), 70-73.

Wood, G. H. (1992). *Schools that work.* New York: Plume.

Further Reading

Altwerger, B. (1987). Whole language: What's new? *The Reading Teacher, 41,* 144-154.

Ames, C. (1990). Classrooms: Goals, structures, and student motivation. *Journal of Educational Psychology, 84*(3), 261-271.

Barzun, J. (1992). *Begin here: The forgotten conditions of teaching and learning.* Chicago: University of Chicago Press.

Batson, C. (1987). Prosocial motivation: Is it ever truly altruistic? *Advances in Experimental Social Psychology, 20,* 65-122.

Beacham, M. (1990, December). How good teachers make students believe in themselves. *The Executive Educator, 12*(12), 16-17.

Bennett, T. (1994). *Meramec Valley R-III connections project survey.* Fulton, MO: William Woods College.

Bird, L. B. (1989). *Becoming a whole language school: The Fair Oaks story.* Katonah, NY: Richard C. Owens.

Brendtro, L., & Ness, A. (1983). *Re-educating troubled youth.* New York: Aldine.

Brodinsky, B., & Keough, K. E. (1989). *Students at risk: Problems and solutions.* Arlington, VA: American Association of School Administrators.

Buncombe, F., & Peetoom, A. (1988). *Literature-based learning: One school's journey.* Richmond Hill, Ontario: Scholastic.

Center for Educational Innovation. (1992). *To design a new generation of American Schools.* New York: Author.

Combs, A. W. (1982). Affective education or none at all. *Educational Leadership, 37*(7), 495-497.

Comer, J. P. (1992, September). Educating students outside the mainstream. *The Education Digest, 58*(1), 28-30.

Edelman, M. (1989). Children at risk. *Proceedings of the Academy of Political Science, 27*(2), 20-30.

Edmonds, R. (1986). Characteristics of effective schools. In U. Neisser (Ed.), *The school achievement of minority children* (pp. 93-104). Hillsdale, NJ: Lawrence Erlbaum.

Elkind, D. (1974). *Children and adolescents: Interpretive essays on Jean Piaget.* New York: Oxford University Press.

Elkind, D. (1984). *All grown up and no place to go.* Reading, MA: Addison-Wesley.

Enz, C. A. (1986). *Power and shared values in the corporate culture.* Ann Arbor: University of Michigan Research Press.

Evans, T. (1997, Winter). The tools of encouragement. *Reaching Today's Youth—The Community Circle of Caring Journal, 1*(2), 18-22.

Fizzell, R., & Raywid, M. (1997, Winter). If alternative schools are the answer . . . What's the question? *Reaching Today's Youth—The Community Circle of Caring Journal, 1*(2), 7-9.

Forman, G., & Kuschner, D. (1977). *The child's construction of knowledge: Piaget for teaching children.* Belmont, CA: Wadsworth.

Forman, G., & Pufall, P. B. (Eds.). (1988). *Constructivism in the computer age.* Hillsdale, NJ: Lawrence Erlbaum.

Freeland, S. (1986). Dropouts: Who and why? *Education USA, 1,* 139-141.

Fulwiler, T., & Young, A. (Eds.) (1982). *Language connections: Writing and reading across the curriculum.* Urbana, IL: National Council of Teachers of English.

Gardner, H. (1991). *The unschooled mind: How children think and how schools should teach.* New York: Basic Books.

Glasser, W. (1986). *Control theory in the classroom.* New York: Harper & Row.

Goldstein, A. P. (1990). *Delinquents on delinquency.* Champaign, IL: Research Press.

Goldstein, A. P. (1991). *Delinquent gangs.* Champaign, IL: Research Press.

Goldstein, A. P., & Huff, C. R. (Eds.). (1993). *The gang intervention handbook.* Champaign, IL: Research Press.

Goodman, K., Goodman, Y. M., & Hood, W. J. (1989). *The whole language evaluation book.* Portsmouth, NH: Heinemann.

Grant, G. (1988). *The world we created at Hamilton High.* Cambridge, MA: Harvard University Press.

Graves, D. H. (1985). All children can write. *Learning Disabilities Focus, 1,* 36-43.

Grennon, J. (1984). Making sense of student thinking. *Educational Leadership, 42,* 11-18.

Guild, P. B., & Garger, S. (1985). *Marching to different drummers.* Alexandria, VA: Association for Supervision and Curriculum Development.

Hahn, A. (1987). Reaching out to America's dropouts: What to do? *Phi Delta Kappan, 69*(4), 256-263.

Hill, H. D. (1989). *Effective strategies for teaching minority students.* Bloomington, IN: National Education Service.

Hobbs, N. (1982). *The troubled and troubling child.* San Francisco: Jossey-Bass.

Jalongo, M. R. (1991). *The role of the teacher in the 21st century: An insider's view.* Bloomington, IN: National Educational Service.

Joyce, B. R., Hersh, R. H., & McKibbon, M. (1983). *The structure of school improvement.* New York: Longman.

Kagan, D. M. (1990). How schools alienate students at risk: A model for examining proximal classroom variables. *Educational Psychology, 25,* 105-125.

Kohn, A. (1992). *The case against competition* (rev. ed.). Boston: Houghton Mifflin.

Lerner, R., & Galambos, N. (1984). *Experiencing adolescents.* New York: Garland.

Lewis, C. C., Shaps, E., & Watson, M. (1995, March). Beyond the pendulum: Creating challenging and caring schools. *Phi Delta Kappan,* pp. 547-554.

Lewis, C. C., Shaps, E., & Watson, M. S. (1996, September). The caring classroom's academic edge. *Educational Leadership, 54*(1), 16-21.

Lewis, K. S. (1986, September). Reforming secondary schools: A critique and agenda for administrators. *Educational Leadership, 44*(1), pp. 33-36.

Marlowe, J. (1992, October). Six easy lessons. *The Executive Educator,* pp. 28-30.

Molnar, A., & Lindquist, B. (1989). *Changing problem behavior in schools.* San Francisco: Jossey-Bass.

Morris, R. C., (Ed.). (1992). *Solving the problems of youth at risk: Involving parents and community resources.* Lancaster, PA: Technomic.

National Commission on Excellence in Education. (1982). *A nation at risk: The need for education reform.* Washington, DC: Government Printing Office.

Neale, D. C., Bailey, W. J., & Ross, B. E. (1981). *Strategies for school improvement.* Boston: Allyn & Bacon.

Newman, J. (1984). *The craft of children's writing.* Richmond Hill, Ontario: Scholastic.

Ogden, E. H., & Germinario, V. (1988). *The at-risk student.* Lancaster, PA: Technomic.

Osborne, J. K., & Brynes, D. A. (1990). Identifying gifted and talented students in an alternative learning center. *Gifted Child Quarterly, 34*(4), 143-145.

Paulson, F. L., Paulson, P. R., & Meyer, C. A. (1991, February) What makes a portfolio a portfolio? *Educational Leadership, 48,* 51-53.

Robbins, P. (1989, November) Implementing whole language: Bridging children and books. *Educational Leadership, 47*(6), 50-54.

Rossi, R. J., & Stringfield, S. C. (1995, September). What we must do for students placed at risk. *Phi Delta Kappan, 77*(1), 73-76.

Rowland, S. (1984). *The inquiring classroom: An approach to understanding children's learning.* London: Falmer.

Saracho, O. N., & Gerstly, C. K. (1992). *Learning differences among at-risk minority students.* In H. C. Waxman, J. Walker de Felix, J. E. Anderson, & H. P. Baptiste, Jr. (Eds.), *Students at risk in at risk schools.* Newbury Park, CA: Corwin.

Schorr, L. (1988). *Within our reach: Breaking the cycle of disadvantage.* New York: Doubleday.

Searson, S. (1971). *The culture of the school and the problem of change.* Boston: Allyn & Bacon.

Shore, R. (1995, February). How one high school improved school climate. *Educational Leadership,* pp. 76-78.

Small, G. (1989, September/October). Keeping students in school: Software as an effective tool. *Media and Methods, 26*(1), 46-47.

U.S. Bureau of the Census. (1992). *Statistical abstract of the United States* (108th ed.). Washington, DC: Government Printing Office.

Vorrath, H., & Brendtro, L. (1985). *Positive peer culture* (2nd ed.). New York: Aldine.

Waterman, R. (1990). *Adhocracy: The power to change.* Knoxville, TN: Whittle Direct Books.

Weaver, C. (1990). *Understanding whole language.* Portsmouth, NH: Heinemann.

Werner, C. (1996). *The state of America's children, yearbook, 1996.* Washington, DC: Children's Defense Fund.

Whittaker, J. (1979). *Caring for troubled children.* San Francisco: Jossey-Bass.

Woolfolk, A. E. (1983). *Educational psychology* (5th ed.). Boston: Allyn & Bacon.

Young, T. (1990). *Public alternative education.* New York: Teachers College Press.